The CPEC and SDGs in Pakistan

"In this study, Sadia Sulaiman Bukhari thoughtfully and carefully examines the effects of the China-Pakistan Economic Corridor on the people of Pakistan. It is easy to talk about geopolitics, but it is hard work to understand the implication of those politics in the lives of real people. This book helps us understand Chinese economic statecraft and the trajectory of contemporary Pakistan. It consequently will be an important resource for a wide-range of experts."

—Christopher Clary, *Associate Professor of Political Science, University at Albany, State University of New York*

"This study presents a novel approach to understand the impact of China-Pakistan Economic Corridor (CPEC) on the lives of common people across Pakistan. The study touches several issue areas that have not been discussed before e.g. CPEC influencing the health and education sectors and that too in the rural areas. While CPEC remains engulfed with its own share of geopolitical challenges, this study examines its possible contribution for attainment of SDGs 3, 4, and 8 in both urban and rural Pakistan. This makes it really worth reading by both policy analysts as also by academics and practitioners in the field of human development."

—Swaran Singh, *Professor, School of International Studies, Jawaharlal Nehru University, New Delhi*

Sadia Sulaiman

The CPEC and SDGs in Pakistan

Measuring the Impact on Common Lives

Sadia Sulaiman
Area Study Centre for Africa, North
and South America
Quaid-i-Azam University
Islamabad, Pakistan

ISBN 978-3-031-65578-4   ISBN 978-3-031-65579-1 (eBook)
https://doi.org/10.1007/978-3-031-65579-1

© The Editor(s) (if applicable) and The Author(s), under exclusive license to Springer Nature Switzerland AG 2024

This work is subject to copyright. All rights are solely and exclusively licensed by the Publisher, whether the whole or part of the material is concerned, specifically the rights of translation, reprinting, reuse of illustrations, recitation, broadcasting, reproduction on microfilms or in any other physical way, and transmission or information storage and retrieval, electronic adaptation, computer software, or by similar or dissimilar methodology now known or hereafter developed.
The use of general descriptive names, registered names, trademarks, service marks, etc. in this publication does not imply, even in the absence of a specific statement, that such names are exempt from the relevant protective laws and regulations and therefore free for general use.
The publisher, the authors and the editors are safe to assume that the advice and information in this book are believed to be true and accurate at the date of publication. Neither the publisher nor the authors or the editors give a warranty, expressed or implied, with respect to the material contained herein or for any errors or omissions that may have been made. The publisher remains neutral with regard to jurisdictional claims in published maps and institutional affiliations.

Cover credit: © Harvey Loake

This Palgrave Macmillan imprint is published by the registered company Springer Nature Switzerland AG
The registered company address is: Gewerbestrasse 11, 6330 Cham, Switzerland

If disposing of this product, please recycle the paper.

Foreword

It is hard to overstate the significance of the Belt and Road Initiative (BRI), Beijing's massive, globe-girdling transport corridor. It might have lost some momentum in recent years, but it remains one of the more consequential developments in international relations over the last decade—because of its scale, its reach, and its impact on strategic competition, among other things. The significance of BRI extends to the China-Pakistan Economic Corridor (CPEC), one of its most active and operationalized components. CPEC, like the broader BRI, has received plenty of attention from the scholarly and analytical communities. They've applied a wide lens to CPEC, with studies of its history, its motivations, its projects, its successes and failures, its outcomes, its impacts on local communities and foreign policy, and so much more.[1]

---

[1] Some examples of this scholarship include Andrew Small, "Returning to the Shadows: China, Pakistan, and the Fate of CPEC," German Marshall Fund and Georgetown Law, September 2020, Report No. 16, https://www.gmfus.org/sites/default/files/Small%2520-%2520China%2520Pakistan%2520CPEC%2520-%252023%2520September.pdf; Arif Rafiq, "The China-Pakistan Economic Corridor: Barriers and Impact," U.S. Institute of Peace, October 25, 2017, https://www.usip.org/publications/2017/10/china-pakistan-economic-corridor; and "China-Pakistan Economic Corridor: Opportunities and Risks," International Crisis Group, Asia Report No. 297, June 29, 2018, https://www.crisisgroup.org/sites/default/files/297-china-pakistan-economic-corridor-opportunities-and-risks_0.pdf.

What has been lacking to this point, however, is a serious study that links CPEC outcomes to normative frameworks focused around ideal development goals—chief among them the United Nations Sustainable Development Goals (SDGs). This is what makes the study that follows so novel, and important.

When gauging the impacts of large investment projects in other countries, a core focus area is how they affect local communities and the broader country in question. Are local jobs created? Are energy and other resources generated? Are technologies transferred? More broadly, are growth and development increased? Studies of large-scale agricultural investments in sub-Saharan Africa, Southeast Asia, and Latin America during and soon after the global food crisis in 2007 and 2008 (when agriculture was a highly attractive investment) show that on many fronts, the positive spillover effects of foreign investments were often woefully lacking.[2]

In more recent years, however, infrastructure investments have ramped up in a big way, in great part because of BRI. Pakistan, because of CPEC, has been a major target of such projects. In assessing the impacts of CPEC on local communities and the country on the whole, it helps to focus the analysis around a set of preferred development outcomes that enjoy a strong international consensus—and the SDGs are a great place to start.

This study's focus on CPEC and SDGs serves three useful purposes. First, it adds something new and important to the large body of scholarship on Pakistan's relationship with China. CPEC is a defining feature of the contemporary Pakistan-China partnership—one of Pakistan's closest and most important ally—and any new analysis on CPEC will make a novel contribution. Indeed, most of the existing scholarship on CPEC looks at it from the lens of geopolitics, or security threats, or broader social and economic impacts—but not from the angle of whether CPEC helps or hinders the pursuit of SDGs.

Second, the study makes a useful contribution to contemporary international development policy analysis. Given its scale, CPEC is not only a case study of BRI; it's also a case study of development assistance more broadly: A major and ambitious undertaking envisioned to create roads, rails, ports, and electricity, among other public goods (and because of

---

[2] Michael Kugelman and Susan L. Levenstein, eds., *The Global Farms Race: Land Grabs, Agriculture Investment, and the Scramble for Food Security* (Washington, DC: Island Press, 2012).

the strategic considerations that motivate Beijing's thinking on CPEC, it will never be mistaken for a charitable project). How countries and companies do foreign investment, and how that investment plays out in the countries receiving it, is a fundamental line of inquiry for development studies. Consequently, this report offers takeaways that can serve as lessons learned for other large foreign development projects, and not just CPEC.

Finally, this study provides important data points to inform a robust debate tied to great power competition. As U.S.-China tensions have intensified in recent years, U.S. officials have sought to counter Chinese investment projects by coming up with their own. These range from clean energy infrastructure initiatives sponsored by Washington's International Development Finance Corporation (DFC), to multilateral projects such as the G7's Build Back Better World and most recently the India-Middle East-Europe Economic Corridor—as well as legacy (albeit unfinished) projects like the Turkmenistan-Afghanistan-Pakistan-India gas pipeline.

None of these initiatives—including DFC investments, the only one of the above examples that has actually been operationalized in any way—can hold a candle to the scale and breadth of China's foreign infrastructure projects. However, Washington distinguishes its investments from China's by drawing a contrast: While Beijing's investments are opaque, lacking in positive spillover effects, and simply not good deals, Washington's are more transparent, beneficial for local communities, and make good financial sense for host governments. It's an argument that U.S. officials make frequently. They don't call for countries not to take on Chinese investments; they argue that the U.S. can provide better alternatives.

This position was first articulated publicly in 2019 by Alice Wells, then the top U.S. official at the State Department focused on South Asia. She contended that the sustainable growth model embodied by CPEC was, well, unsustainable—and that the U.S. can do it better.[3] This position is closely tethered to the values-based dimensions of the U.S. Indo Pacific Strategy, which calls for Washington to act in ways that promote a "free and open" and "rules-based order." The implication is that while U.S. investment projects can help advance this vision, CPEC does not.

---

[3] "A Conversation with Ambassador Alice Wells on the China-Pakistan Economic Corridor," Wilson Center, November 19, 2019, https://www.wilsoncenter.org/event/conversation-ambassador-alice-wells-the-china-pakistan-economic-corridor.

Of course, many commentators—and not just in Beijing and Islamabad—have pushed back hard against this argument. One can reasonably argue that the U.S. hasn't yet produced a critical mass of new overseas infrastructure investments, making it difficult to offer substantive assessments of them, much less to compare them to Chinese projects. However, this study puts the U.S. assertion to the test by offering its own assessment of what impacts CPEC has had on SDGs focused on health, education, and economic growth (SDGs No. 3, 4, and 8, respectively).

SDGs are indeed a useful yardstick to measure the social and economic impacts of large-scale foreign investments. Given the most recent trends in such investments, there are two additional SDGs that will deserve increasing amounts of attention in the coming years: affordable and clean energy, and climate action (SDGs No. 7 and 13, respectively). BRI and CPEC have increasingly emphasized clean energy investments in recent years; in 2021, Beijing pledged to no longer fund investments in coal power abroad and to ramp up efforts to deploy capital for renewable energy. The DFC's investments are mostly focused on clean energy infrastructure. This is, of course, a consequence of the very simple and sobering fact that development needs are increasingly tied to the growing threat of climate change and its harsh effects.

One can talk about investments that focus on both hard (roads and rails) and soft (fiber optics, healthcare) infrastructure. The former provides core building blocks for growth and development. The latter helps make economic growth stronger and more sustainable. But we'll soon be hearing a lot more about green infrastructure: Investments that help people better manage the inevitable threat of climate change. In the coming years, these investments will become all the more important—as will the need to produce assessments, such as this one, to see if the investments are generating the type of preferred (green) development outcomes that local communities will badly need.

Michael Kugelman
Director of the South Asia
Institute at the Wilson Center
Washington, DC, USA

Acknowledgements

This research project is supported by the British Academy's Sustainable Development Program (SDP2/100222), supported under the UK Government's Global Challenges Research Fund. I am indebted to British Academy for the generous grant which made this research and writing possible. Their support was instrumental in bringing this project to fruition.

I would like to express my sincere gratitude to all those who contributed to the completion of this research successfully. First and foremost, I would like to express my heartfelt gratitude to Dr Rudra Chaudhry, for his unwavering support throughout this project. His guidance and encouragement were invaluable and greatly contributed to the successful completion of this years' long project and research. I am equally grateful to Dr Deep Pal whose expertise and insights were instrumental in shaping the analytical framework and methodology of this research, which greatly enriched the content of this book. I am grateful to all my colleagues who helped in designing and editing the study to give it the best possible shape.

My researchers, Maryam and Mamoona, need special appreciation who worked tirelessly in the field during the challenging times of the COVID-19 lockdown to collect the data for this research. My researchers never gave up during the tiring and tense environment due to pandemic. Their dedication and perseverance in ensuring the completion of this research despite the difficult circumstances are truly commendable. All of my interviewees also deserve a special thanks who took time out to answer queries, build my knowledge and understanding and to clear my doubts that led to successful completion of the research study.

Additionally, I am indebted to my friends and family, especially my kids, Fatimah, Hyder, Kazem and Asad, for their patience, understanding and encouragement during the research and writing process. Their belief in me kept me motivated to see this project through to completion. I would also like to thank the readers for their interest in this work. It is my hope that this project will contribute to a better understanding of this important initiative. Finally, I would like to thank the Palgrave MacMillan editorial team for their meticulous editing and dedication. Their commitment to excellence has helped shape this work into its final form, ensuring its clarity and impact.

Contents

1 Introduction ... 1
The Impact of the CPEC on Communities ... 4
Methodology ... 5
What Determines How SDGs Are Delivered? ... 6
Existing Infrastructure ... 6
Access to Existing Infrastructure ... 9
Projection about the Impact of the Projects ... 9
Actual Impact of the Projects ... 10
Response from Stakeholders: Civil Society and Citizens ... 10
Miscellaneous Factors ... 10
The CPEC in Urban and Rural Pakistan ... 11
Organization of the Study ... 12

2 CPEC in Pakistan: The Journey Hitherto ... 17
Introduction ... 17
Key Areas under CPEC ... 19
CPEC: Key Challenges and Concerns ... 24
   Security Challenges to CPEC ... 24
   Political Imbroglio in Pakistan and CPEC ... 26
   Economic Woes of Pakistan and Development on CPEC ... 27
   Local Discontent ... 28

3	**SDGs and Health, Education and Economic Well Being in Pakistan**	33
	Introduction	33
	Analyzing the Progress on SDGs in Pakistan	35
	SDG 3 in Pakistan	35
	SDG 4 in Pakistan	37
	SDG 8 in Pakistan	39
4	**CPEC and the Delivery of Public Goods in Azad Jammu and Kashmir**	45
	Introduction	45
	The Neelum-Jhelum Hydroelectric Project	46
	Infrastructure	47
	Claims About the Project, and the Reality	48
	Response from Citizens and Civil Society	49
	Kohala Hydropower Project	49
	Infrastructure	50
	Claims About the Project, and the Reality	51
	Response from Citizens and Civil Society	51
5	**CPEC and the Delivery of Public Goods in Khyber Pakhtunkhwa**	59
	Introduction	59
	Rashakai Special Economic Zone	60
	Infrastructure	61
	Claims About the Project, and the Reality	62
	Response from Citizens and Civil Society	64
	Peshawar–D.I. Khan Motorway	65
	Infrastructure	65
	Claims About the Project, and the Reality	66
	Response from Citizens and Civil Society	67
6	**CPEC and the Delivery of Public Goods in Punjab**	73
	Introduction	73
	Sahiwal Coal Power Plant Project	74
	Infrastructure	74
	Claims About the Project, and the Reality	75
	Response from Citizens and Civil Society	76
	Orange Line Metro Train Project	78
	Infrastructure	78

		Claims About the Project, and the Reality	79
		Response from Citizens and Civil Society	80
7		**Conclusion and Recommendations**	87
		SDG Delivery Is Not a Core Objective for CPEC Projects at Present	88
		CPEC Projects Aid SDG 8 More Than SDG 3 or SDG 4	88
		For SDG 3 and SDG 4, the Promised Effect of CPEC Projects Does Not Match the Reality	89
		CPEC Projects Affect Urban and Rural Areas Differently	90
		Policy Recommendations	90

Index 95

ABBREVIATIONS

AJK	Azad Jammu and Kashmir
BLA	Baluchistan Liberation Army
BISP	Benazir Income Support Program
BRI	Belt and Road Initiative
CPEC	China-Pakistan Economic Corridor
CSAIL	Three Gorges South Asia Investment Ltd.
CGGC	China Gezhouba Group Co. Ltd.
CMEC	China Machinery Engineering Corporation
CPHC	China-Pakistan Health Corridor
CRBC	China Road & Bridge Corporation
EPA	Environment Protection Agency
GB	Gilgit Baltistan
JWG	Joint Working Group
KHP	Kohala Hydropower Project
KP	Khyber Pakhtunkhwa
KPEZDMC	KP Economic Zone Development and Management Company
NJHP	Neelum-Jhelum Hydroelectric Project
NMDs	Newly Merged Tribal Districts
OLMT	Orange Line Metro Train
OSC	Out of School Children
PMLN	Pakistan Muslim League – Nawaz
PTI	Pakistan Tehrik-i-Insaf
RSEZ	Rashakai Special Economic Zone
SDGs	Sustainable Development Goals
SNGPL	Sui Northern Gas Pipelines Limited
SSGC	Sui Southern Gas Company

TTP	Tehrik-i-Taliban Pakistan
UN	United Nations
UHC	Universal Health Coverage
USD	US Dollar
WAPDA	Water and Power Development Authority
WHO	World Health Organization

List of Figures

Fig. 2.1	Major Terrorist Attacks on Chinese Nationals	25
Fig. 3.1	Out of School Children in Pakistan (*Source* Kashif Abbasi, "Government Turns its Back on Education", *Dawn*, January 23, 2024, https://www.dawn.com/news/1807937)	39

List of Tables

Table 1.1	Study Indicators	7
Table 2.1	Phases of the China–Pakistan Economic Corridor	19
Table 2.2	Special Economic Zones under the CPEC	22
Table 3.1	SDGs in Pakistan	34
Table 4.1	Delivery of Public Goods in AJK	53
Table 5.1	Development Phases of Rashakai Special Economic Zone	62
Table 5.2	Delivery of Public Goods in KP	68
Table 6.1	Delivery of Public Goods in Punjab	81
Table 7.1	Impact of CPEC Projects on SDGs	91

CHAPTER 1

Introduction

Abstract The purpose of this chapter is to introduce the readers with the aim of the study which is to analyze the impact of the China-Pakistan-Economic-Corridor (CPEC) on the common lives across rural and urban areas of Pakistan. The study adopts a unique approach to gauge the changes in lives of common people due to CPEC through measuring CPEC's impacts on SDG 3 (Good Health and Well Being), SDG 4 (Quality Education) and SDG 8 (Economic Well Being). The key findings of the study indicate towards the attainment of SDG 8 to some extent while having nominal impact of this grand development initiative on SDGs 3 and 4. It recommends more synchronization between the development goals of CPEC with SDGs so as to make this initiative truly impactful at grassroot level.

Keywords CPEC · Pakistan · China · Sustainable Development Goals (SDGs) · Development

The USD 60 billion+ China–Pakistan Economic Corridor (CPEC) initiative signed between the two countries in 2015 is expected to transform the lives of people across Pakistan by promoting bilateral connectivity and construction, through easing bilateral investment and trade and by advancing regional connectivity as well as encouraging people-to-people contact.[1] At the end of its first phase, the corridor now spans all four provinces and two regions in Pakistan with projects spanning transportation networks, energy projects, and special economic zones. Flagship projects like the Orange Line Metro Train in Lahore and the Gwadar Port in Baluchistan along with several others have been completed while others are in various stages of development.

The CPEC has garnered significant scholarly attention, both for its role as a predicted key node in China's flagship Belt and Road Initiative (BRI) as well as its importance to regional geopolitics. However, considering the scale and geographical spread of CPEC projects in Pakistan, it is important to examine the effects of the initiative on the socioeconomic fabric of the country. For instance, how have CPEC projects impacted the lives of local communities? How is the question of the delivery of public goods connected with the development of these projects? How does the impact change under different demographic and geographic conditions? And what role do government agencies, the private sector, civil society, and local populations play in how these public goods are delivered?

This study aims to address these questions by examining the development of CPEC projects across Pakistan and their impact on the daily lives of people as reflected in three crucial Sustainable Development Goals (SDGs) encapsulated by the United Nations—good health and wellbeing, inclusive and equitable quality education, and decent work and economic growth (SDGs 3, 4, and 8, respectively). Decent work, a healthy and productive life, and quality education enable sustainable development. They each represent integral elements of the 2030 Agenda for Sustainable Development and are broadly rooted in the targets of the other fourteen goals. The provision of these public goods requires collaboration, partnership, sustained attention, and continued dedication of all stakeholders—local, national, and international. While the universality of Agenda 2030 is essential, it is important to mark the variation in challenges all countries face. Modifications in the traditional way of life affect development, and this study aims to understand the influence of major infrastructure projects as big as CPEC on the daily lives of people.

While the initiative has been usually assessed through a top-down, geopolitical lens, there are other aspects to understand and explore. This study takes a step in this direction, where the socioeconomic impacts of the CPEC have been examined through a bottom-up approach to look at the changes that CPEC projects may have brought on the ground in the lives of common people. The study evaluates the impact of projects ranging from highways, metro rail links, industrial parks, and energy projects to the upgradation of transport and communication facilities across Pakistan. Linking the CPEC with SDG outcomes is significant not only as a measure of the former's socioeconomic impact but also to look at the bigger picture—the role that major infrastructure initiatives can play in the country's development policy.

The study examines the impact of the CPEC across urban and rural Pakistan, highlighting the varying impact of its projects with changes in geography, demography, level of existing public goods, and sociopolitical awareness. In their early phases, CPEC projects were concentrated in urban Pakistan—Punjab and Sindh along with the Gwadar Port in Baluchistan—while in recent years, projects have been launched in rural parts of the country, including Khyber Pakhtunkhwa (KP), Baluchistan, Gilgit-Baltistan (GB), and Azad Jammu and Kashmir (AJK). While urban areas are somewhat better equipped with health, education, and economic opportunities, rapid urbanization has increased the need for socioeconomic development across the country. Pakistan has approached these challenges with a two-pronged strategy—first, identifying and mitigating challenges to public service delivery in cities and second, improving the delivery of public goods and increasing economic opportunities in rural areas to make them attractive to residents.[2] Since CPEC projects are key to development and urbanization across Pakistan, this study not only examines the status of public goods delivery in focus areas before and after the operationalization of projects, but it also investigates the various perspectives and expectations in the local communities connected to these projects.

Both Pakistan and China have committed to having the SDGs at the core of their development policies. However, this study finds that development goals that affect daily life most closely—the need for healthcare and education along with economic opportunities—seldom feature among the core objectives of CPEC projects. This is despite an understanding, both at the popular and elite level, that synchronizing CPEC objectives with SDG delivery is crucial to meet challenges to the development landscape in Pakistan. In most cases, there is a greater focus on SDG 8, especially in rural areas, where economic opportunities are limited. However, the study finds that there is often a gap between the proposed or promised employment opportunities, which are subject to political posturing, and the reality on the ground, which is dictated by the skillsets needed for the project. There is a greater focus on investing in the local community under newer projects. However, there is still a long way to go before CPEC projects consider the socioeconomic development of local communities as important as meeting the overall objectives of addressing national development requirements.

THE IMPACT OF THE CPEC ON COMMUNITIES

While the CPEC has attracted abundant scholarly focus, most studies have approached the subject either with a geopolitical lens or from the perspective of the Pakistan-China relationship.[3] The role of the Gwadar Port project, for instance, in providing China and Pakistan with better connectivity for both economic and strategic purposes, has been analyzed extensively.[4] A significant part of the literature has also focused on Pakistan's challenges that the CPEC might help address, including requirements of industrial development, energy deficit, poor transportation infrastructure and connectivity, and economic debt.[5]

While examining the role that the CPEC can play in addressing the country's economic and development necessities, few studies have engaged with the experience of the communities that are impacted. Some studies have explored the potential of the projects or how they are perceived. A 2018 study suggests that successful implementation of the CPEC can contribute to the delivery of SDGs not only in Pakistan but across Western China, Central Asia, and the Middle East.[6] Another study from the same year examining the role of perception of the future impact of the projects found that the more the residents perceived the effects of the projects positively, the more they were likely to support the CPEC.[7] Similarly, a 2020 study examining the role of CPEC projects in Baluchistan found that local communities perceived infrastructure improvements to be beneficial to their wellbeing.[8] According to another study conducted the same year, women, especially those in rural Pakistan, were found particularly hopeful that the CPEC would improve their quality of life, not just by providing more employment opportunities, but more comprehensively, through the overall development of the areas that they live in.[9] Local communities expect these projects to improve communication linkages, make energy available, as well as provide better health and education facilities while eradicating poverty.[10]

The survey of existing scholarship suggests that the study of the connection between completed or ongoing CPEC projects on SDGs is still in a nascent stage. Fewer studies have engaged with local and affected communities across the country, providing an on-ground assessment from sites where CPEC projects are underway. This study expects to address this gap with evidence from six project locations across both urban and rural areas in Pakistan.

Methodology

Where most studies have analyzed the CPEC from a big-picture perspective driven by elite decision-making and geopolitical considerations, this project strives to employ a bottom-up approach to investigate the effects of the initiative on the ground. The study chose six projects namely; Kohala Hydropower Project, Neelum-Jhelum Hydropower Plant project, Sahiwal Coal Power Plant, Lahore Orange Line Metro Train, Rashakai Special Economic Zone and Peshawar—Dera Ismail Khal (D.I.Khan) Motorway project. The selection of the projects was based on purposive sampling, where projects from both urban (Punjab) and rural areas (KP and AJK) were selected. KP and AJK have remained under studied in the discussion on CPEC and most importantly in the last few years there was an increasing focus in these two regions, hence this study opted for detailed analysis of four mega projects from both KP and AJK to fill the existing gap in literature. Moreover, this analysis proves to be very timely for the relevant stakeholders to get a clear picture of how to make these projects more people-centric for improving common lives in the rural areas of Pakistan.

Using case studies of these six projects from across the country, the study triangulates data from a variety of sources, both primary and secondary, to arrive at a coherent narrative about the impact of CPEC projects on everyday life. As often is the case with research on the CPEC, the study faced a scarcity of consistent ground-level data, often because the projects are ongoing. Additionally, there is often explicit hesitation in talking about the CPEC even on the part of local communities and those who are most likely to be impacted by these mega projects. In some cases, the remoteness of the terrain has contributed to the difficulties in gathering data, especially during the COVID-19 pandemic. The study attempts to overcome this limitation by rigorous triangulation and plotting broad trend lines. The insights in the study have been sourced through a comprehensive review of open-source data and literature on daily life along CPEC projects across Pakistan.

The project employs insights from four national and local newspapers between 2013 and 2020. To ensure sufficient coverage of the CPEC and a diversity of views, *Jang*, *Nawai Waqt*, and *Ausaf* from Urdu newspapers and the *Express Tribune* from English newspapers were selected for monitoring. However, the study also uses latest possible information from other newspapers to present an updated picture of the development. Beyond these, data collected from government departments, policy documents, and records, including those from the National Assembly (the lower house of Pakistan's parliament) and the Senate (the upper house of the parliament), have contributed to the study.

In addition, the study has been informed by around fifty in-depth stakeholder interviews conducted between October 2020 and July 2022. Interviewees include members of civil society, academics, retired and serving government officials, and, most crucially, residents from communities potentially affected by CPEC projects. For an overall perspective on the CPEC and its impact, a detailed literature review was conducted involving more than a hundred research journal articles and online research reports compiled by various global think tanks from the initiation of the CPEC project in 2013 till the end of 2022.

What Determines How SDGs Are Delivered?

The study examines six separate sets of indicators through which SDG deliveries are connected to CPEC projects. These are selected keeping in view the goals of the CPEC in general and of the six projects that are the subject of this study (Table 1.1).

Existing Infrastructure

A region's infrastructure is the fundamental vehicle for service delivery and achieving development goals. Studying existing infrastructure in areas close to CPEC projects offers an understanding of possible opportunities available to locals. The number of hospitals or educational institutions being constructed or upgraded near CPEC projects, or the construction of toll plazas, rest areas, and tuck shops on the highways constructed under CPEC, can indicate possible changes in the lives and livelihoods of local people. Beyond physical infrastructure, the study also examines the accessibility of these facilities for local populations. In the case of SDG 8,

Table 1.1 Study Indicators

SDG / Indicators	SDG 3: good health and wellbeing	SDG 4: inclusive and equitable quality education	SDG 8: Decent work and economic growth
Existing infrastructure	– What is the equipment and staffing situation in health facilities around the project location? – Are electricity supply and telecommunication access consistent and sufficient?	– What is the equipment, syllabus, and staffing situation in schools around the project location? – Are electricity supply and telecommunication access consistent and sufficient?	– What is the state of financial infrastructure around the project location? – What are the employment opportunities in public organizations and the private—organized and unorganized—sector? – Are electricity supply and telecommunication access consistent and sufficient?
Access to existing infrastructure	– How near and affordable are health facilities? – What communication and transport services are available to people? – How have the projects changed affordability and access to health facilities, if at all?	– How near and accessible are schools? – What communication and transport services are available to people? – How have the projects changed affordability and access to educational facilities, if at all?	– How near and accessible are banks, ATMs, and other financial services? – What communication and transport services are available to people? – How have the projects changed affordability and access to economic opportunities, if at all?
State's (Pakistan) projections of project impact	– Is addressing/improving health a consideration for the project? – What are the government's claims about the impact of the project on health? – How do the results so far stand up to the government's claims?	– Is addressing/improving education a consideration for the project? – What are the government's claims about the impact of the project on education? – How do the results so far stand up to the government's claims?	– Is addressing/improving economic opportunities a consideration for the project? – What are the government's claims about the impact of the project on economic opportunities? – How do the results so far stand up to the government's claims?

(continued)

Table 1.1 (continued)

SDG / Indicators	SDG 3: good health and wellbeing	SDG 4: inclusive and equitable quality education	SDG 8: Decent work and economic growth
Actual impact of project	– How has the construction and functioning of the CPEC projects affected existing health indicators? – What new opportunities for healthcare have the projects offered?	– How has the construction and functioning of the CPEC projects affected existing education indicators? – What new opportunities for education have the projects offered?	– How has the construction and functioning of the CPEC projects affected existing economic opportunities? – What new opportunities for economic activity have the projects offered?
Citizens/civil society's response	– How have civil society and citizens responded to the announcement of the CPEC project? – How have they responded to the negative or positive change brought about by the construction or functioning of the CPEC project? – How aware are they of the potential of CPEC projects to help achieve health outcomes? – How has the government responded to concerns raised by these parties?	– How have civil society and citizens responded to the announcement of the CPEC project? – How have they responded to the negative or positive change brought about by the construction or functioning of the CPEC project? – How aware are they of the potential of CPEC projects to help achieve educational outcomes? – How has the government responded to concerns raised by these parties?	– How have civil society and citizens responded to the announcement of the CPEC project? – How have they responded to the negative or positive change brought about by the construction or functioning of the CPEC project? – How aware are they of the potential of CPEC projects to contribute toward an increase in economic activity? – How has the government responded to concerns raised by these parties?
Miscellaneous factors	– How has gender impacted health outcomes? – Has the construction of projects led to displacement and migration? – How has the project and its construction impacted the environment?	– How has gender impacted educational outcomes? – Has the construction of projects led to displacement and migration? – How has the project and its construction impacted the environment?	– How has gender impacted economic activity? – Has the construction of projects led to displacement and migration? – How has the project and its construction impacted the environment?

for instance, this refers not just to the establishment of physical infrastructure but also to whether they add to the potential for gainful employment. Additionally, the state of physical connectivity infrastructures, such as roads, airways, alternative routes, available transportation, and digital facilities, including communication services, was also evaluated.

Access to Existing Infrastructure

A survey of available infrastructure needs to also consider the means to access these facilities to determine whether people can access services available to them. Access to infrastructure needs to be evaluated along two parameters—physical proximity and affordability. For instance, while the OLMT project has eased pressure on public transport in Lahore, residents have pointed out the lack of feeder transportation facilities to access the metro stations.[11] Similarly, the location of the Sahiwal Coal Power Plant has made travel between villages in the area more difficult and expensive for locals. This indicates that access to facilities is an important consideration in determining the efficacy of infrastructure in contributing to the lives of people. Since this study considers projects in rural as well as urban areas of Pakistan, factors like terrain and weather have also been considered to the extent that they are relevant to the execution and functioning of CPEC projects in impacting everyday life.

Projection about the Impact of the Projects

Another important consideration for this study is the stated objective of CPEC projects on SDG delivery. According to Pakistani and Chinese agencies associated with the initiative, a key expected outcome from the CPEC is an overall improvement of infrastructure along with an acceleration of urbanization across the country. Facilities like hospitals, schools, marketplaces, clean drinking water, and paved roads are key to an improvement in living standards. How does the development of these facilities feature in the priorities of the agencies in charge of CPEC projects? The study analyzes publicly available data, such as statements and policy documents, to examine this question.

Actual Impact of the Projects

A continuation of the stated objectives of CPEC projects is a study of the actual impact of these initiatives. Interviews with stakeholders including residents of areas with active and completed CPEC projects were aimed at better understanding how people perceive or expect their living standards to change pre and post CPEC. For instance, the first phase of the CPEC focused on improving connectivity across urban and rural Pakistan through a network of roads and railway tracks. Key project in this phase include the OLMT. The study assesses the changes in the delivery of health, education, and economic opportunities as experienced by local communities before and after these projects were operationalized.

Response from Stakeholders: Civil Society and Citizens

The role of civil society is crucial to this study to understand the aspirations of communities that are affected by CPEC projects, and more so, the gap between the objectives of the projects and their actual impact. Action from civil society organizations, including protests, public meetings, and campaigns, is useful in gauging people's attitudes toward the projects as well as expectations of health and education services and better economic opportunities. Similarly, local journalists are key in highlighting ground-level contentions and sentiments. The role of civil society is especially important in capturing the voice of marginalized populations. For example, in Azad Jammu and Kashmir (AJK), the Kohala Hydropower Plant saw considerable protests from locals concerned about the environmental impact of the project.[12]

Miscellaneous Factors

Certain miscellaneous variables cut across SDGs in their impact on the lives of communities in the vicinity of CPEC projects and need to be included in this study. These span across SDGs as well as state or non-state efforts to deliver public goods. For instance, sociopolitical factors like political instability, elections, corruption, protests, civilian unrest, and terrorism, even when disconnected from CPEC projects, have the potential to affect the delivery of health and education opportunities as well as employment. Displacement and migration, whether state-led or otherwise, are important factors as they change the requirement for public goods in particular regions and have the potential to leave a permanent impact on the socioeconomic fabric of the region. Similarly, gender is a factor, as the unavailability of opportunities disproportionately impacts women's health, education, and employment, and needs to be examined as such.

THE CPEC IN URBAN AND RURAL PAKISTAN

Examining projects from both rural and urban Pakistan offers significant analytical advantages because of critical differences in approach, expectations, and understanding of development issues by the elites and the population in these areas. The difference has to do with multiple factors—most importantly, with the status of the availability of public goods. Changes in the accessibility of public goods as CPEC projects progress are further influenced by levels of education and awareness, political empowerment, and the role of civil society. According to the 2017 census, 63% of Pakistan's population lives in rural areas. These areas are often sidelined in major development initiatives and face multiple challenges including a lack of education and health infrastructure, poor facilities for sanitation and potable water, a dearth of economic opportunities, and a lack of infrastructure and connectivity with urban areas that can offer better circumstances. Additionally, around 35% of Pakistan's rural population lives below the subsistence level where social services and basic facilities are absent.[13]

Coexisting with this reality and connected to it is the fact that Pakistan is the fastest urbanizing country in South Asia.[14] Half of the country's population is expected to be living in cities by 2025.[15] This development comes with its challenges—most significantly, those related to scaling up urban infrastructure, including public transport and connectivity, health, housing, and education; availability of social and economic opportunities; and improvement in governance with well-thought-out, long-term inclusive policies. These are some of the critical questions facing Pakistan's major cities where public service delivery is struggling to keep up with the rate and scale of expansion.

For the next few decades, the CPEC will be a major contributor to the process of urbanization with its involvement in improving digital and physical communication infrastructure and focus on industrialization.

In separately analyzing CPEC projects in rural and urban Pakistan, this study examines the demand for adequate and effective delivery of public services and how CPEC projects are reacting to the expectations. The urban projects considered in the study include the Sahiwal Coal Power Plant Project and the Orange Line Metro Train (OLMT) project, both in Punjab. The rural projects include the Rashakai Special Economic Zone and Peshawar-Dera Ismail Khan Road projects from KP province and the Neelum-Jhelum Hydropower Plant (NJHP) and Kohala Hydropower Plant in AJK.

The NJHP project in AJK included in this study is different from the others as it is not officially a part of the CPEC. However, the project is one of the earliest instances of China and Pakistan working together on infrastructure projects and continues to be a model for CPEC projects. It was started in January 2008 after a consortium of Chinese companies was awarded the contract.[16] Several issues examined by this study first emerged during this project, including those of the land acquisition and allotment process, the role of civil society and the agency of local communities, and how economic development engages with questions of the lives and livelihoods of residents. An analysis of the impact of NJHP, therefore, helps set up the questions employed to examine the role of CPEC projects in the delivery of SDGs 3, 4, and 8.

Organization of the Study

The Study is divided into five chapters followed by a conclusion that provides policy recommendations as well. The first chapter profiles CPEC in Pakistan since its formal inauguration in April 2015. The chapter provides update on the projects that have been completed or ongoing in various fields namely, energy, transport and infrastructure, special economic zones (SEZs), Gwadar, Social and Economic Development and agriculture, science and technology and IT. The chapter also brings into focus the key challenges that hindered the smooth execution of the project. After having a broader idea of the CPEC layout across Pakistan, the study provides an insight into SDGs 3, 4 and 8 in Pakistan and evaluate what has been achieved and missed out while pursuing these SDGs at policy level. Chapters 3–5 provide details of case studies selected from AJK, Khyber Pakhtunkhwa (KP) and Punjab respectively. In conclusion, after discussion of the key findings of the research some important recommendations have been proposed.

Notes

1. "$62 Billion Infrastructural and Energy Projects being Developed under CPEC: Scholars," *The News*, December 17, 2021, https://www.thenews.com.pk/print/917411-62-billion-infrastructural-and-energy-projects-being-developed-under-cpec-scholars; "CPEC Mission and Vision," CPEC Official Website, accessed February 5, 2022, https://cpec.gov.pk/vision-mission/3#:~:text=To%20improve%20the%20lives%20of,people%20contact%20for%20regional%20connectivity.
2. For further details, see Michael Kugelman, ed., *Pakistan's Runaway Urbanization: What Can be Done?* (Washington: Wilson Center, 2014): 2–6.
3. Zhang Zhexin, "The Belt and Road Initiative: China's New Geopolitical Strategy?" *China Quarterly of International Strategic Studies* 4, no. 3 (October 2018): 327–43; Agnieszka Nitza-Makowska, "China–Pakistan Economic Corridor and Sustainable Development Goal Implementation in Pakistan: Fostering Sustainable Connectivity in a Fragile Context?" *Journal of Peacebuilding & Development* 15, no. 3 (2020): 377–82.
4. Hamzah Rifaat and Tridivesh Singh Main, "The China-Pakistan Economic Corridor Strategic Rationales, External Perspectives, and Challenges to Effective Implementation," A Visiting Fellow Working Paper, Stimson Centre, 2016, https://www.stimson.org/wp-content/files/file-attachments/The%20China-Pakistan%20Economic%20Corridor%20-%20Final.pdf; Muhammad Ijaz Latif and Muhammad Tayyab Zia, "Strategic Dimensions of CPEC: Role of Regional and International Powers," *Journal of Business and Social Review in Emerging Economies* 6, no. 4 (2020): 1561–69; Fakhar Hussain, "Geostrategic Imperatives of Gwadar Port for China," *The Korean Journal of International Studies* 18, no. 2 (August 2020): 145–67; Matt Harris, "The Strategic Importance of Gawadar Port," *ThinkCPIC* (blog), China-Pak Investment Corporation, February 2019, https://www.cpicglobal.com/the-strategic-importance-of-gwadar-port/; Jeremy Garlick, "Deconstructing the China–Pakistan Economic Corridor: Pipe Dreams Versus Geopolitical Realities," *Journal of Contemporary China* 27, no. 112 (2018): 519–33.

5. Muhammad Tayyab Safdar, "The Local Roots of Chinese Engagement in Pakistan," Carnegie Endowment, June 2, 2021, https://carnegieendowment.org/2021/06/02/local-roots-of-chinese-engagement-in-pakistan-pub-84668; see also Zahid Khan, "The China-Pakistan Economic Corridor: Economic Rational and Key Challenges," *China Quarterly of International Strategic Studies* 5, no. 2, 249–65; Muhammad Faisal Sultan, Israr Ahmed, and Muhammad Raghib Zafar, "Measuring the Impact of China Pakistan Economic Corridor on the Socio-Economic Aspects of Pakistan: A Quantitative Research Highlighting the Public Opinion," *Journal of Economics and Sustainable Development* 8, no. 23 (2017).
6. Murad Ali, "The China Pakistan Economic Corridor: Tapping Potential to Achieve the 2030 Agenda in Pakistan," *China Quarterly of International Strategic Studies* 4, no. 2 (2018): 301–25.
7. Shamsa Kanwal, Ren Chong, and Hameed Pitaffi, "Support for CPEC Development in Pakistan: A Local Community Perspective Using Social Exchange Theory," *Journal of Public Affairs* 19, no. 1 (2018).
8. Yunpeng Sun, Usman Ghani, Abdul Hameed Pitaf, and Tahir Islam, "Social-Cultural Impacts of China-Pakistan Economic Corridor on the Well-Being of Local Community," *The Journal of Transportation and Land Use* 13, no. 1 (2020): 605–24; see also Khawar Abbas, "Socio-economic impacts of China Pakistan Economic Corridor (CPEC) at Community Level. A Case Study of Gwadar Pakistan," 2019, https://uia.brage.unit.no/uia-xmlui/bitstream/handle/11250/2616202/Abbas,%20Khawar.pdf?sequence=1.
9. Ahmad Saad, Mariah Ijaz, Muhammad Usman Asghar, and Liu Yamin, "China-Pakistan Economic Corridor and Its Impact on Rural Development and Human Life Sustainability. Observations from Rural Women," *PLOS ONE*, October 2020, https://journals.plos.org/plosone/article?id=10.1371/journal.pone.0239546.
10. Massarat Abid and Ayesha Ashfaq, "CPEC: Challenges and Opportunities for Pakistan," *Journal of Pakistan Vision* 16, no. 2 (2015): 142–69; Muhammad Faisal Sultan, Israr Ahmed, and Muhammad Raghib Zafar, "Measuring the Impact of China Pakistan Economic

Corridor on the Socio-Economic Aspects of Pakistan: A Quantitative Research Highlighting the Public Opinion," *Journal of Economics and Sustainable Development* 8, no. 23 (2017); Liaqat Ali, Jianing Mi, Mussawar Shah, Sayed Jamal Shah, Salim Khan, and Kausar BiBi, "The Potential Socio-Economic Impact of China Pakistan Economic Corridor," *Asian Development Policy Review* 5, no. 4 (2017): 191–98; Shehryar Khan and Guijian Liu, "Socioeconomic and Policy Impacts of China Pakistan Economic Corridor on Khyber Pakhtunkhwa," *Environmental Management and Sustainable Development* 8, no. 1 (2019): 57.
11. Interview with Stakeholder D3, February 2021.
12. Tariq Naqash, "AJK Government Sets Conditions for Kohala Power Project," *Dawn*, July 15, 2019, https://www.dawn.com/news/1494144.
13. Saad, Ijaz, Asghar, and Yamin, "China-Pakistan Economic Corridor and Its Impact on Rural Development and Human Life Sustainability. Observations from Rural Women.".
14. Ignacio Artaza, "Urbanisation in Pakistan," *The Express Tribune*, June 5, 2019, https://tribune.com.pk/story/1986926/urbanisation-in-pakistan.
15. "Is Rapid Urbanization Ruining Pakistan's Cities?" *DW*, May 10, 2020, https://www.dw.com/en/is-rapid-urbanization-making-pakistans-cities-less-livable/a-55162735.
16. Shafqat Ali, "Pakistan's CPEC Parliamentary Committee Visits Neelum Jhelum Hydel Power Project," *Gwadar Pro*, November 15, 2021, https://gwadarpro.pk/1460092414912294914/pakistan-cpec-parliamentary-committee-visits-neelum-jehlum-hydel-power-project.

CHAPTER 2

CPEC in Pakistan: The Journey Hitherto

Abstract This chapter provides an overview of the China-Pakistan-Economic-Corridor (CPEC) since its initiation in 2015 as a landmark development project between China and Pakistan. Major areas of cooperation include energy sector, transportation infrastructure, Special Economic Zones (SEZs), Information Technology (IT), science and technology, agriculture and socio-economic development. The chapter identifies some key challenges faced by this project such as; security concerns, politicization of this project, inflated expectations of common people and the debt burden due to the CPEC energy projects.

Keywords CPEC · Energy · Special Economic Zones (SEZs) · Information Technology (IT) · Socio-Economic Development · Gwadar

INTRODUCTION

The China-Pakistan-Economic-Corridor (CPEC) is a significant infrastructure and economic development project. It covers important fields such as energy cooperation, transportation infrastructure, construction of Special Economic Zones (SEZs), Information Technology, Science and Technology, Agricultural and Socio-economic development. It is aimed at connecting China and Pakistan and broader Central and West

© The Author(s), under exclusive license to Springer Nature Switzerland AG 2024
S. Sulaiman, *The CPEC and SDGs in Pakistan*,
https://doi.org/10.1007/978-3-031-65579-1_2

Asian region through a transport and trade corridor. The CPEC is expected to improve Pakistan's economic potential through improved connectivity, uninterrupted availability of energy for industrial growth and through creation of better socio-economic opportunities. However, it has also faced criticism for its environmental implications, its role in Pakistan's debt crisis, its sluggish pace of development hampering other development objectives and due to lack of transparency in its agreements.

According to Ministry of Planning, Development and Special Initiatives of Pakistan, since its inception in 2015, 36 projects, worth USD 24 billion have been completed and 22 projects, worth USD 5 billion, are in progress.[1] The CPEC projects have contributed to job creation, generating approximately 200,000 employment opportunities for locals in Pakistan.[2] Along with it, the CPEC has "facilitated the production of 6,000 megawatts of electric power, the construction of 510 kilometers of highways, and the expansion of the national transmission network by 886 kilometers."[3] At the time of this writing, the CPEC is in its second phase with emphasis upon industrial advancement through SEZs, collaboration in the agriculture sector, and other socioeconomic development initiatives.[4]

The Joint Cooperation Committee (JCC), with 11 subordinate Joint Working Groups (JWG), provides administrative framework for CPEC implementation, for monitoring the progress of various projects and deciding about inclusion of more projects into the ambit of CPEC. The JCC is co-chaired by the Planning Minister of Pakistan and the Chairman of the National Development and Reform Commission of China. The JCC meetings are held periodically to review the progress on CPEC projects.

The CPEC projects were divided into the short, medium, and long term to be completed by 2030. Various projects are designated within each phase as discussed in Table 2.1.

The CPEC covers a wide range of projects, essential for the economic growth and making this corridor beneficial for both China and Pakistan. However, despite its uniqueness and vitality, the project witnessed delay in actual implementation and its delivery of public good is yet to be seen. The following sections provide details about the various projects and also identify some major problems faced in the implementation of CPEC projects across Pakistan.

Table 2.1 Phases of the China–Pakistan Economic Corridor[5]

Phases	Objectives	Duration
Phase One (Early Harvest Projects)	To remove key economic bottlenecks, especially in energy and infrastructure, to pave the way for development	2015–2019/2020
Phase Two (Medium-term projects)	To boost industrialization, socioeconomic development, trade promotion, and agricultural growth	2020–2025
Phase Three (Long-term projects)	To complete all projects in various fields to reap the benefits of the CPEC	2026–2030

KEY AREAS UNDER CPEC

a. Energy

Pakistan has faced a severe energy crisis for the past many years, characterized by frequent power outages, insufficient capacity of power generation, persistently increasing circular debt in power sector and subsequent high electricity prices. The energy crisis hit its peak in 2011 when Pakistan was faced with more than 6000 megawatts shortfall.[6] The situation remained critical affecting millions of people across the country and especially hitting hard the country's industrial capacity. For instance, more than five hundred industrial units in Faisalabad were closed due to prolonged energy outages, hence paralyzing production and exacerbating unemployment.[7] Several factors contribute to energy crisis in Pakistan including, heavy reliance on imported fuels and subsequent vulnerability to global price shocks, inadequate investment in energy sector, inefficiencies and corruption in the power sector and lack of proper policy orientation.[8]

In order to address this crisis, in the first phase of CPEC energy projects were given priority to better support the energy requirements of Pakistan and prepare it for the second phase of CPEC, where the major focus would be on rapid industrialization and trade through establishment of SEZs. Among the initial 22 priority projects more than half were energy projects to construct new energy infrastructure and also to upgrade the existing ones for better energy supply across country.[9] In the first ten years of CPEC, seven coal-fired power generation plants, four wind power generation projects, one hydropower and one solar power projects have been completed. These projects helped in creating approximately 34,000 jobs. According to the data of the Ministry of Planning, Development and Special Initiatives, as part of these CPEC energy projects 14,016 people have been given jobs in Sindh, 8,511 people in Punjab, 5,200 in Baluchistan and 4,000 in Khyber Pakhtunkhwa (KP).[10]

Under CPEC, nine power projects in Sindh, two in Punjab, one in Baluchistan and one on the Jhelum River have been completed while one transmission line project between Sindh and Punjab have been completed at a cost of USD 2.54 billion.[11] According to Economic Survey of Pakistan, the country has the capacity to generate 41,000 megawatts of electricity, including 10,592 megawatts of hydropower, 24,095 megawatts of thermal power, 3,530 megawatts of nuclear power. Under CPEC, 8,020 megawatts of electricity has been added to the national grid which means 20% of the electricity included in the current national grid is from the projects that have been completed in the first 10 years of CPEC.[12]

While CPEC projects have helped increase Pakistan's electricity generation capacity it has also contributed towards circular debt in energy sector of Pakistan. However, it is worth mentioning that Pakistan's debt crisis is very complex and requires comprehensive reforms, including improvement in governance, identification and ramifications of inefficiencies, increase in revenue collection and rationalization of subsidies.

b. Transport and Infrastructure

Transportation infrastructure plays a significant role in economic development of any country and Pakistan is no exception in this regard. Pakistan's geography with its diverse terrain and long distance between major cities and ports makes a well-developed transportation network essential for trade, commerce and social cohesion. Along with roads, Pakistan has two ports Karachi and Port Qasim that are fully functional. The Gwadar port has been recently added to the ports of Pakistan. There is still a need to increase air connectivity within the country and airport infrastructure to meet growing passenger and cargo traffic needs.[13]

Within this context, the CPEC priorities include significant investment in transportation infrastructure. In the early harvest projects of CPEC, six mega infrastructure projects were completed including, Havelian-Thakot section of KKH, Multan-Sukkur (M-5) Motorway, Hakla-Dera Ismail

Khan (D.I.Khan) Motorway, Optical Fiber Cable, Eastbay Expressway and Orange Line Metro Train (OLMT). Furthermore, on western alignment of CPEC, work on different sections is under progress. Since, most of these highways pass through the far-flung areas of Pakistan, it has opened those areas for business which will bring prosperity.[14] To modernize the Pakistan Railway system under CPEC, the Main Line-1 (ML-1) project is in final stages of agreement. This project will help in upgradation and dualization of 1733 km of railway track from Peshawar to Karachi.[15] All these projects are vital for improving and enhancing connectivity and bringing significant economic benefits to Pakistan.

c. *Special Economic Zones (SEZs)*

The SEZs constitute an important segment of the second phase of CPEC. SEZs have been approved in all four provinces of Pakistan with the aim to improve and encourage industrialization, technology transfer, making use of local raw materials, employment creation and revenue generation. The Board of Investment of Pakistan is the competent authority to approve SEZS in the four provinces. However, it takes all decisions in consultation with the provinces.[16]

Initially, nine SEZs were approved as detailed in the Table 2.2. Pakistan is currently working on five out of these nine priority SEZs, which include Allama Iqbal Industrial City in Faisalabad, Dhabeji SEZ in Sindh, Rashakai Special Economic Zone in KP and Boston Special Economic Zone in Baluchistan. The status of the remaining four SEZs is yet to be determined.

The total land allocation for SEZs account for approximately 10.029 acres out of which 52% has been already allotted with the proposed investment of PKR 633.9 billion.[17] Meanwhile two state companies, Sui Northern Gas Pipelines Limited (SNGPL) and Sui Southern Gas Company (SSGC) are tasked with providing gas connection to these five priority SEZs. Within this context, SNGPL has planned to execute a 29 km pipeline project for supply of 30 million cubic feet per day gas to Rashakai Special Economic Zone. According to Annual Development Plan of 2020–2021, the SSGC would supply of 13.5 and 13 million cubic feet per day gas to Dhabeji Special Economic Zone and Bin Qasim Industrial Park in Karachi respectively.[18]

Table 2.2 Special Economic Zones under the CPEC

Name of SEZ	Location	Status
Rashakai Special Economic Zone	Nowshera	Under construction
Dhabeji Special Economic Zone	Thatta	Under construction
Bostan Special Economic Zone	Quetta	Under construction
Allama Iqbal Industrial City	Faisalabad	Under construction
ICT Model Industrial Zone	Islamabad	In pipeline
Mirpur Industrial Zone	Mirpur, AJK	In pipeline
Mohmand Marble City	Mohmand Tribal District, Khyber Pakhtunkhwa	In pipeline
Moqpondass Special Economic Zone	Gilgit-Baltistan	In pipeline
Industrail Park on Pakistan Steel Mills Land	Port Qasim, Karachi	In pipeline

Despite all these efforts the overall pace of development on these SEZs is slower than expected. Issues pertaining to lack of connectivity infrastructure, complexities involving land acquisition, challenges of creating policy and regulatory framework and lack of investment due to security reasons have all contributed to the slow pace of development on this front.

d. *Gwadar Port*

Gwadar port, located in the Southwestern province of Baluchistan in Pakistan, holds strategic significance under CPEC. It is strategically located at the entrance of Persian Gulf with proximity to Strait of Hormuz, which is world's most important oil chokepoints. The Gwadar port provides China with a shorter route for its energy imports bypassing the Malacca Strait. Under CPEC, Gwadar is envisioned as a hub of trade and economic activity which would play a vital role in connecting China and Pakistan both with Central Aia, Middle East and African continent. Despite being the focal point of CPEC, the overall pace of progress on the development of this project is very slow. Reportedly by 2022, only four projects could be completed including USD 4 million Gwadar Smart Port City Master Plan, the Physical Infrastructure of Gwadar Port and the Free Zone Phase-1 costing USD 300 million and Pak-China Technical and Vocational Institute that has been built with a USD 10 million Chinese grant.[19] In December 2023, two China-donated projects, including a seawater desalination plant and the upgrade of the Pak-China Friendship Hospital, were inaugurated in Gwadar. The desalination plant will provide 5,000 tons per day of potable water to help address a severe drinking water shortage, while the Pak-China Friendship Hospital boosted its capacity to 150 beds from the original 50.[20]

The development of Gwadar Port and CPEC could not receive the anticipated appreciation by everyone. The issues of displacement of local fishing communities and environmental costs are key concerns of the local people that led towards Haq Do Tehreek (Gwadar Rights Movement) in the area recently.[21] The movement, led by Maulana Hidayat-ur-Rehman, demanded an end to illegal trawling, ease in doing informal business with neighboring Iran, reduction in number of security checkpoints in the area, and access to clean drinking water, hospitals, and electricity.[22] On top of that the uncertain and futile security situation has resulted in shaking the confidence of the investors and slowed down the progress on this project.

e. Social and Economic Development

As the CPEC has entered its second phase after 2020, the focus has shifted to socioeconomic development and industrial and agricultural cooperation. The JCC has identified twenty-seven projects in six sectors including agriculture, health, education, drinking water and supply, poverty alleviation, and vocational and technical education to be initiated under socio-economic development sector. These projects are expected to contribute to the attainment of SDGs, which have largely been missing in the conversation surrounding the role of the CPEC in advancing development in Pakistan.[23] For instance, in the first phase, while the Kohala Hydropower Plant, Sahiwal Coal Power Plant, and Thar Engro Coal Power Project promised to construct rural roads and create education and health facilities as part of the project, such initiatives were eventually scrapped.

f. *Agriculture, Science and Technology and IT*

Agriculture, Science and Technology and IT are some crucial areas of cooperation between Beijing and Islamabad under the umbrella of CPEC.

Advancing cooperation in the agricultural sector, China Machinery Engineering Corporation (CMEC) and Sichuan Litong Food Group have established a company and carried out a red chili contract farming project in 2021, with model farms across Punjab.[24] Pakistan needs to use Chinese technology and technical assistance to cope with climate change and food security challenges. Similarly, in the realm of IT development, a fiber optical cable project was successfully completed and it is helping to improve the telecom industry in Pakistan. Both the countries are committed "to strengthen cooperation on building digital economic infrastructure, digitization, the Internet, satellite navigation, the Internet of things (IoT), computing infrastructure like data centers, cloud computing, and smart infrastructure including artificial intelligence and 5G Networks."[25] In this regard a Joint Working Group on Information Technology Cooperation has been established to strengthen bilateral cooperation in the IT industry and focus on the development of an innovative and pragmatic China-Pakistan digital corridor.[26]

CPEC: Key Challenges and Concerns

The CPEC when started in 2015, it received positive response from the citizens of Pakistan as general euphoria prevailed with hopes of its positive impacts on people's lives. However, the project has faced multiple challenges that have affected its growth and also affected its pace. Consequently, several CPEC projects could not be completed on time. There are multiple reasons or challenges that are hindering the smooth execution and implementation of CPEC and this section takes stock of these challenges.

Security Challenges to CPEC

The CPEC project started amidst the most critical time period in the history of Pakistan, when the country was reeling with the fatal consequences of the post-9/11 War on Terror. To quell the terrorist threat, Operation Zarb-e-Azab was launched by Pakistan army in 2014 and it took a few years time to tackle this challenge in Pakistan. Meanwhile, Pakistan raised a special security task force for the protection of CPEC and the project despite speculation remained safe from direct security threats. However, due to the fragile security situation across Pakistan the project could not be initiated as planned in some areas, especially that of KP and Newly Merged Tribal districts (NMDs).

The security of CPEC is the responsibility of the Pakistan military, which has set up two special security infantry divisions for this purpose. One division, the 34 Light Infantry Division, is based in Chilas for the security of Gilgit-Baltistan (GB) and KP. The other division, 44 Infantry Division is based in Gwadar for its security.[27]

It was primarily in Baluchistan province that the CPEC came under attack by the militants several time. It is a fact that despite decades-long separatist conflict in Baluchistan and resultant insecurity, China has invested extensively in Gwadar port. Local residents, however, have protested that the development projects are marginalizing, rather than benefiting Gwadar's inhabitants—many of whom still lack access to water and electricity. While capitalizing on these sentiments, the militant and separatist groups have recently started to attack the Chinese nationals involved in various projects of CPEC.[28] Figure 2.1 provides details of key recent terrorist attacks against Chinese nationals especially after the US withdrawal from Afghanistan, which emboldened the Tehrik-i-Taliban Pakistan (TTP). It in return supported the Baloch separatists and militants against CPEC.

Baluchistan Liberation Army (BLA) is one of the militant outfits in Baluchistan that is actively involved in the terrorist attacks against CPEC and it has claimed the responsibility for almost all major attacks on CPEC. One of the BLA's first major anti-China attacks was on the

Terrorist Attack	Terrorist Attack	Terrorist Attack
• Date of Attack: April 2022 • Key Target: Chinese Confucious Institute • Location: Karachi, Sindh • Responsibility Claimed: Majeed Brigade, Armed Wing of BLA	• Date of Attack: August 2023 • Key Target: Chinese Nationals • Location: Gwader • Responsibility Claimed: Balochistan Liberation Army (BLA)	• Date of Attack: March 2024 • Key Target: Gwader Port Authority Complex • Location: Gwader Balochistan • Responsibility Claimed: Majeed Brigade, Armed wing of BLA

Fig. 2.1 Major Terrorist Attacks on Chinese Nationals

Chinese consulate in Karachi on November 23, 2018.[29] Chinese officials continue to urge Pakistan to take strong actions to protect Chinese nationals and projects, emphasizing the importance of maintaining cooperation between the two countries. In response, Pakistan has promised to strengthen security measures for Chinese nationals and projects, including increasing intelligence sharing and enhancing security standards.[30]

Political Imbroglio in Pakistan and CPEC

Another key challenge for CPEC is political instability in Pakistan, which has, to an extent, diverted governmental attention to other matters than long-term developmental projects. The incumbent Pakistan Muslim League-Nawaz (PML-N) government was the one who always take pride in initiation of CPEC under the leadership of Muhammad Nawaz Sharif back in 2015. When Imran Khan's Pakistan Tehrik-i-Insaf (PTI) came into power in 2018, the CPEC witnessed a stalemate due to the mounting tensions between the PTI and Chinese government. The tensions between the PTI and Chinese government started in 2014, when PTI as opposition party was staging protest in Islamabad which delayed Chinese President Xi Jinpiang's visit and consequently the signing ceremony of the CPEC got delayed. After coming into power in 2018, PTI had frequently expressed reservations over the CPEC western and eastern routes, raised concerns about its transparency, and accused the federal government for the misuse of funds. Although Imran Khan's politics targeted the ruling PML-N and on occasion he sought to clarify that he was not against CPEC, his rivals interpreted his policies as opposed to Chinese projects—an impression that many circles in China accepted.[31]

Khan was found critical of Sharif's policy of giving priority to Punjab and Sindh to shore up his political base in the region and ignoring the smaller provinces of KP and Baluchistan. However, when Khan came into power and after immediate criticism of CPEC and plans to take the CPEC into parliament to open up its details, he mellowed down his criticism. Khan diverted the CPEC investment into KP to shore up support for his political party in KP—a region with support for Imran Khan. During his tenure the military took the center stage in CPEC authority that further shook the confidence of potential investor looking at the fragile political scenario in Pakistan.[32]

The PTI government had to leave the Parliament after a successful vote of no confidence and PML-N government under the PM Shehbaz Sharif commenced in. Immediately after coming into power again the PML-N government initiated the work on CPEC. In March 2024, Federal Minister of Planning, Development & Special Initiatives, Ahsan Iqbal, and the Chinese envoy, Jiang Zaidong, both sides agreed to expedite the second phase of CPEC and establish a working group on five new economic corridors, including the Corridor of Job Creation, Corridor of Innovation, Corridor of Green Energy, and Inclusive Regional Development.[33]

Economic Woes of Pakistan and Development on CPEC

The financial strain and lack of clarity and direction in Pakistan's economic policy is another key reason slowing CPEC's progress. The initial estimation of costs on CPEC has increased multifold and Pakistan while managing its current account deficit always found struggling to secure funds for its share. This has led to project delays, like the stalled Gwadar LNG terminal, initially funded by Pakistan but now awaiting Chinese investment. China is also facing economic headwinds and has opted for stricter lending policies, which meant less readily available financing for CPEC, further impacting project timelines. "The financial constraints cast a long shadow on CPEC's completion, demanding innovative solutions and flexible financing models to bridge the funding gap and propel the project forward."[34]

Another aspect of the economic hurdles affecting the growth and pace of CPEC is the debt induced by this project, especially in the energy sector. Pakistan is among the top recipients of China's infrastructure and energy investments; however Islamabad now owes nearly one-third of its external debt to Beijing. It is a lamentable fact that benefits of CPEC for the Pakistani people have been limited and remained confined to a few particular projects, however the burden of public debt and payments to Chinese companies has increased, hence leading towards public discontent with this project. According to a report by US-based research lab AidData in 2021, most Chinese development financing in Pakistan between 2000 and 2017 came as loans given at commercial rates. "Experts say that to lessen the debt burden stemming from CPEC, Pakistan must find ways to efficiently use the energy and infrastructure it acquired through the mega-project and strengthen domestic production and exports."[35]

The core of the CPEC-led debt crisis is considered to be the murky terms and conditions of this project with less clarity as how it would cost Pakistan in terms of economic spending and growth. As of early 2023, Pakistan's external debt crossed USD100 billion and more than USD 30 billion is owed to China. There is a need to introduce broad based political and economic reforms and transparency in the deals with China in future in order to reap maximum benefits out of CPEC.

Local Discontent

While the economic impact of CPEC is evident, it is crucial to address challenges and concerns associated with the initiative. In this context, socio-economic and environmental challenges, such as the displacement of local communities and ecological impacts of large-scale projects, require careful consideration. Balancing local and foreign employment is another challenge, with the need to ensure that the benefits of job creation are equitably distributed among the population.

The climate vulnerability of Pakistan requires diligent implementation of environmental protection laws and the Chinese experience could be a valuable source of guidance. However, the government seems to be prioritizing development without paying attention to environmental security. According to Asian Development Bank, the energy projects under CPEC has dire consequences for the environment. For example, every 10 GW electricity production would intensify CO_2 emissions. Moreover, the ash handling and disposal problems for coal-fired power plants like the one in Sahiwal, Punjab would increase the intensity of smog in the province, which struggles with it every year.[36] Some of the potential environmental issues such as deforestation due to infrastructural development and ecological disruption need immediate attention by both China and Pakistan to avoid negative fallouts of this project.

Addressing community concerns and grievances is paramount for the sustainable success of CPEC. Open and transparent communication between project stakeholders and local communities is essential to mitigate potential tensions and build a harmonious relationship. Striking a balance between economic development and social and environmental responsibility is a delicate task that necessitates thoughtful policies and proactive community engagement.[37]

Notes

1. "36 Projects Completed So Far Under CPEC: Senate Informed," *Associated Press of Pakistan*, January 1, 2024, https://www.app.com.pk/national/36-projects-completed-so-far-under-cpec-senate-informed/.
2. "CPEC Projects Generate Jobs and Energy as China and Pakistan Celebrate 10-Year Partnership," China Pakistan Economic Corridor, April 17, 2023, https://cpecinfo.com/cpec-projects-generate-jobs-and-energy-as-china-and-pakistan-celebrate-10-year-partnership/.
3. "CPEC Projects Granted $25b Direct Investment," *The Express Tribune*, July 10, 2023, https://tribune.com.pk/story/2425529/cpec-projects-garnered-25b-direct-investment.
4. Hasmatullah Khan, Asif Iqbal Dawar and Ruqia, "A Decade of China-Pakistan Economic Corridor: An Explorative Study of its Role in the Economic and Political Development of Pakistan," *Journal of Infrastructure, Policy and Development* 8, no. 1 (2024): 7 (1–16).
5. See Ministry of Planning, Development, & Special Initiatives, "CPEC Projects Progress Update," https://cpec.gov.pk/progress-update.
6. Murad Ali, "CPEC in Pakistan's Quest for Energy Security: Clarifying Some Misperceptions," *China Quarterly of International Strategic Studies* 7, no. 2 (2021): 181.
7. Michael Kugelman, "Pakistan's Energy Crisis: From Conundrum to Catastrophe," Commentary from Energy Security Program, The National Bureau of Asian Research, March 2013, https://www.nbr.org/publication/pakistans-energy-crisis/.
8. Please see Elizabeth Mills, "Pakistan's Energy Crisis," *Peaceworks*, USIP, No 79, June 2012, https://www.usip.org/sites/default/files/PW79_Pakistans_Energy_Crisis.pdf.
9. Murad Ali, "CPEC in Pakistan's Quest for Energy Security: Clarifying Some Misperceptions," *China Quarterly of International Strategic Studies* 7, no. 2 (2021): 183–84 (179–198).
10. "CPEC Role Instrumental in Meeting Pakistan's Energy Needs," *Dunya News*, August 01, 2023, https://dunyanews.tv/en/Business/743871-CPEC-role-instrumental-in-meeting-Pakistan%E2%80%99s-energy-needs.

11. Ibid.
12. Ibid.
13. Muhammad Suleman Aziz, Muhammad Rahies Khan, Sajid Mehmood, Azmat Ullah Baig, "Overview of Pakistan's Transportation Infrastructure from Future Perspective: A Systematic Literature Review," *Journal of Applied Research and Multidisciplinary Studies* 4, no. 2 (2023): 7–9 (1–25).
14. "Mega Projects of CPEC Completed in Record Time One Year: Ahsan Iqbal," Press Release by Ministry of Planning Development & Special Initiatives, June 2023, https://www.pc.gov.pk/web/press/get_press/1031.
15. Ibid.
16. "Special Economic Zones Vital for Pakistan's Economic Growth: Expert Says," *CPEC Info*, February 13, 2024, https://cpecinfo.com/special-economic-zones-vital-for-pakistans-industrial-growth-under-cpec-expert-says/.
17. "Pakistan Currently Developing Five SEZs, Says SEZA Chief," *The Business Recorder*, December 27, 2022, https://www.brecorder.com/news/40216853.
18. "Government Is Set to Expedite Work on Special Economic Zones under CPEC," *Sindh Economic Zone Management Company*, https://sezmc.gos.pk/government-is-set-to-expedite-work-on-special-economic-zones-sezs-under-cpec/.
19. Shabaz Rana, "Only Three Projects in CPEC Completed," *The Express Tribune*, May 08, 2022, https://tribune.com.pk/story/2355606/only-3-cpec-projects-in-gwadar-completed.
20. Chu Daye and Xie Wenting, "CPEC Running on Fast Lane," *Global Times*, February 22, 2024, https://www.globaltimes.cn/page/202402/1307494.shtml.
21. Syed Fazl-e-Haider, "CPEC at Ten: A Road to Nowhere," *China Brief* 23, no. 19, October 2023, https://jamestown.org/program/cpec-at-ten-a-road-to-nowhere/.
22. Somaiyah Hafeez, "Gwadar's Trial and Tribulations," *The Diplomat*, January 12, 2023, https://thediplomat.com/2023/01/gwadars-trials-and-tribulations/.
23. Atr-un-Nisa, "CPEC and Socio-Economic Development," *Development Advocate Pakistan* 6, no. 4 (2019).

24. Misbah Sabah Malik and Jiang Chao, "Chinese Red Chili Contract Farming Opens Vistas for Development in Pakistan's Agriculture Sector," *Xinhau*, July 01, 2023, https://english.news.cn/202 30701/5785d6311c87499e93e60cc13dacca78/c.html.
25. Please check the Official Website of CPEC, "Information Technology Cooperation under CPEC," https://cpec.gov.pk/information-technology.
26. Ibid.
27. K.N. Pandita, "Tehreek-e-Jihad Pakistan: 'A New Kid on the Block' Emerges as a Big Threat to China's CPEC," *Eurasia Times*, July 23, 2023, https://www.eurasiantimes.com/tehreek-e-jihad-pakistan-the-new-kid-on-the-block-emerges/.
28. Asfandyar, "Another Attack on Chinese Nationals in Pakistan Puts CPEC Back Under Scrutiny," *The Diplomat*, August 15, 2023, https://thediplomat.com/2023/08/another-attack-on-chinese-nationals-in-pakistan-puts-cpec-back-under-scrutiny/.
29. Riccardo Valle and Lucas Webber, "Rising Anti-China Sentiment in Baluchistan Threatens Increased Attacks on Chinese Interests in Pakistan," *Terrorism Monitor* 22, no. 1 (January 2024), https://jamestown.org/program/rising-anti-china-sentiment-in-balochistan-threatens-increased-attacks-on-chinese-interests-in-pakistan/.
30. "Gwader Attack Reignite Security Debate in Pakistan," *Pakistan Observer*, March 21, 2024, https://pakobserver.net/gwadar-attack-reignites-cpec-security-debate-in-pakistan/.
31. Ghulam Ali, "What Next for China-Pakistan Relations?" *The Interpreter*, Lowy Institute, August 15, 2018, https://www.lowyinstitute.org/the-interpreter/what-next-china-pakistan-relations.
32. Reid Standish, "Why China Is Closely Watching the Pakistani Elections?" *Radio Free Europe Radio Liberty (RFERL)*, February 07, 2024, https://www.rferl.org/a/pakistan-elections-china-watching-analysis/32809620.html.
33. "Phase 2 of CPEC Accelerated with New Economic Corridors," *The Express Tribune*, March 23, 2024, https://tribune.com.pk/story/2460230/phase-2-of-cpec-accelerated-with-new-economic-corridors.
34. Oleksandra Mamchii, "10 Big Reasons Why CPEC Is Not Completed Yet," *Best Diplomats*, Blog, February 13, 2024, https://bestdiplomats.org/why-cpec-is-not-completed-yet/.

35. Sarah Zaman, "Is China Responsible for Pakistan's Debt Problem?" *Voice of America*, August 4, 2023, https://www.voanews.com/a/is-china-responsible-for-pakistan-s-debt-problem-/7211897.html.
36. Iram Khalid, Tooba Ahmed and Sami Ullah, "Environmental Impact Assessment of CPEC: A Way Forward for Sustainable Development," *International Journal of Development Issues* 21, no. 1, (2021), https://www.emerald.com/insight/content/doi/10.1108/IJDI-08-2021-0154/full/html#sec004.
37. Shah Khalid, "CPEC's Infrastructure Development and Employment Generation," *Eurasia Review*, March 15, 2024, https://www.eurasiareview.com/22112023-cpecs-infrastructure-development-and-employment-generation-oped/.

CHAPTER 3

SDGs and Health, Education and Economic Well Being in Pakistan

Abstract The purpose of this chapter is to analyze the situation in Pakistan in terms of attainment of SDGs 3, 4 and 8. The SDGs hold utmost importance for a country with low human development indicators like Pakistan. Even though Pakistan was the first country to officially endorse the 2030 Agenda in 2015, the attainment of SDGs remains slow and behind the schedule. The synchronization of the SDGs with development initiatives as big as CPEC can help in quick and effective implementation of the objectives of these two separate agendas with almost similar goals of betterment of the common people.

Keywords Sustainable Development Goals (SDGs) · Health · Education · Economic Well Being · CPEC

INTRODUCTION

Adopted in 2015 by the United Nations (UN), the Sustainable Development Goals (SDGs) are a universal call for global action to ensure peace and prosperity of global community through ensuring actions in 17 key areas including poverty reduction, gender equality, environmental protection and economic well-being. These 17 goals are adopted by all the member countries of the UN—both developed and underdeveloped.

© The Author(s), under exclusive license to Springer Nature Switzerland AG 2024
S. Sulaiman, *The CPEC and SDGs in Pakistan*,
https://doi.org/10.1007/978-3-031-65579-1_3

The SDGs acknowledge "ending poverty and other deprivations must go hand-in-hand with strategies that improve health and education, reduce inequality, and spur economic growth – all while tackling climate change and working to preserve our oceans and forests."[1]

Like the rest of the world, Pakistan committed to the pursuit of these goals as being the first country to officially endorse the 2030 Agenda in 2015. In the same context, a dedicated SDGs Section has been established at the federal level in the Ministry of Planning, Development & Special Initiatives, the same Ministry that is in-charge of the CPEC, for monitoring and coordination as a national coordinating entity to ensure smooth and successful attainment of these goals. A Parliamentary SDGs Secretariat was founded at the National Assembly to do required legislation to help support mainstreaming and localizing the SDGs. Pakistan has categorized the SDGs in three wide-ranging and interconnected sets of priorities intended to address global challenges and foster sustainable development as outlined in Agenda 2030 (Table 3.1).[2]

Table 3.1 SDGs in Pakistan

Priority I Goals	Priority II Goals	Priority III Goals
SDG 2: Zero Hunger	SDG 1: No Poverty	SDG 12: Responsible Consumption and Production
SDG 4: Quality Education	SDG 5: Gender Equality	SDG 13: Climate Action
SDG 6: Clean Water and Sanitation	SDG 9: Industry, Innovation and Infrastructure	SDG 14: Life Below Water
SDG 7: Affordable and Clean Energy	SDG 11: Sustainable Cities and Communities	SDG 15: Life on Land
SDG 8: Decent Work and Economic Growth	SDG 17: Partnerships for the Goals	
SDG 16: Peace, Justice and Strong Institutions	SDG 10: Reduced Inequalities	
SDG 3: Good Health and Well Being		

Analyzing the Progress on SDGs in Pakistan

Despite the ratification of the United Nations goals for sustainable development and poverty reduction by the national legislature as early as 2016, Pakistan faces considerable challenges in meeting these goals.[3] The lack of adequate resources and a coordinated policy to tackle the challenges have resulted in the country dropping in global SDG rankings from 115 in 2016 to 125 in 2022.[4] The following section provides detailed analysis of Pakistan's performance in the pursuit of SDG 3, 4 and 8 so as to overview the impact of CPEC on these SDGs.

SDG 3 in Pakistan

The SDG 3 is Tier One goal in Pakistan and there has been a marginal improvement in recent years, especially in maternal and neonatal mortality rates and immunization numbers in the country.[5] Despite these improvements in healthcare infrastructure and service delivery, Pakistan continues to grapple with significant health challenges, including high maternal and child mortality rates, prevalence of infectious diseases, inadequate access to essential healthcare services, and disparities in healthcare access between urban and rural areas. Limited healthcare financing, weak health systems, and socio-cultural barriers further exacerbate these challenges, particularly for marginalized populations.

In 2018 as part of its efforts to achieve SDG 3, Pakistan signed the UHC2030 Global Compact, committing to advancing universal health coverage (UHC). International donors, while realizing the SDG 3 gap in Pakistan, came together to agree on the Global Action Plan for Healthy Lives and Well-being for All agenda. In this regard the priority areas are primary health care and sustainable financing for health and the World Health Organization (WHO) is leading the program in Pakistan.[6]

Despite prioritization by the government and efforts by global partners, primary health care in Pakistan is marred with several challenges. One of the significant challenges is insufficient funding. Pakistan spends around 38 US Dollars (USD) per capita on healthcare, which is much lower than other developing countries. The insufficient funding affects the overall growth of this sector for the benefit of common people. Issues such as shortage of health infrastructure, medicines, medical equipment, and qualified healthcare professionals are related to the insufficient funding.[7]

Another dimension of the problem is the disparity between rural and urban areas in terms of access to better health facilities. The healthcare resources, including hospitals, clinics, and healthcare professionals, are concentrated in the urban areas, leaving rural areas with inadequate healthcare facilities. Consequently, the rural healthcare system lacks basic medical equipment, diagnostic facilities, and medications for people. All these shortages increase the burden on the infrastructure in cities hence leading to inadequate provision of health facilities, physician shortages, and dissatisfaction among patients.[8] Here the CPEC project can prove to be of utmost importance as it has a major focus on better connectivity linking rural and urban areas. In terms of SDG 3 attainment, this factor is important to see how improved connectivity and mobility is helpful in bringing people closer to healthcare facilities. It is crucial that health facilities are accessible to people in remote and marginalized areas with little transport facilities.[9]

It is a fact that health sector was never a priority area of cooperation under CPEC, however several health facilities were constructed in various project location across Pakistan to cater to the health requirements of the locals. For instance, in December 2023, Pak-China Friendship Hospital was opened in Gwadar under the CPEC.[10] Another example is of a 60-bed THQ hospital at Kahuta that has been supported under CPEC. The hospital is reportedly serving more than 30,000 patients per month.[11] Recently, Pakistan and China have agreed to open a China-Pakistan Health Corridor (CPHC), which comprises of hospitals, nursing and auxiliary medical institutions, research and training centers, IT, and pharmaceutical industries. Through mobile hospitals, laboratories, pharmacies, artificial intelligence, virtual reality and big data, this group shares the achievements of Chinese medical development with Pakistan.[12] Although, it is not part of CPEC at the moment but in future Pakistan may need more such projects especially in alliance with the SDG framework to cater to the needs of common people.

To advance SDG 3 in Pakistan, a multifaceted approach is required. This includes strengthening healthcare infrastructure, expanding the reach of primary healthcare services, improving healthcare financing mechanisms, enhancing health workforce capacity, promoting health education and awareness, and addressing social determinants of health such as poverty, education, and gender inequality. Additionally, leveraging technology and innovation can help improve healthcare delivery and accessibility, particularly in remote areas. In all these areas CPEC can prove beneficial indeed.

SDG 4 in Pakistan

Sustainable Development Goal 4 (SDG 4) signifies inclusive and equitable quality education for all with the aim to promote basic education along with fostering opportunities to learn skills that are essential for sustainable development. In Pakistan, SDG 4 is a Tier-1 goal as education has been prioritized by the government of Pakistan, as enshrined in the country's constitution, emphasizing the Right to Education in Article 25A: "The State shall provide free and compulsory education to all children aged five to sixteen years in such a manner as may be determined by law."[13] However, achieving SDG 4 in Pakistan is not without challenges due to a complex array of factors such as low literacy rates, gender disparities, inadequate infrastructure, lack of funding and disparity within the education system.[14]

According to the 2022 SDG status report, the progress on SDG 4 has remained stagnant overall, with the literacy rate for ages 15–24 at 73%, which is lower than the rest of South Asia.[15] The overall situation of the education sector is not promising rather it is affected by several challenges. According to Pakistan Education Statistics for 2021–2022, there are approximately 26 million Out of School Children (OSC) across country.[16] In the province of Sindh, 15% of children, including a large number of girls, are out of school. In Punjab this figure stands at 14%. The situation is alarming because these two provinces of the country have the highest number of schools, colleges and universities. The worst in terms of educational negligence is Baluchistan where 47% of children are out of school. This means approximately half of the children in this geographically largest province of Pakistan are deprived of their basic right of education. On top of that approximately 1000 primary and secondary schools are temporarily non-functional in settled and merged districts of Baluchistan, whereas 44 others have been permanently closed due to the threat of terrorism. The situation in Khyber-Pakhtunkhwa province is no different: one out of four children in the province are out of school. According to the results of a census survey carried out under the Benazir Income Support Program (BISP) for the year 2021–2022, almost 4.7 million children aged five to 16 are out of school in KP.[17]

The report on Pakistan Education Statistics 2021–2022 revealed that the teacher-student ratio for primary schools in Pakistan stood at 39—there is one instructor for 39 students. Along with it the pupil-school ratio across the country is about 162 and survival rate to Grade-V for Pakistan is 77%.[18]

Despite being the priority area in SDGs, education does not appear as a priority in the budgets of the federal or provincial governments.[19] Pakistan's expenditure on education as a percentage of GDP stood at 1.7% in the fiscal year 2022–2023, which is the lowest in the entire South Asian region.[20] Such financial restraints further affect the quality of education which has been compromised especially in the rural areas with little accessibility to educational institutions and there the quality of education remains compromised, characterized by outdated curricula, poorly trained teachers, and inadequate learning resources.

One important aspect of this problem is the lack of basic facilities that hinder progress in the education sector. For example, approximately 24% of primary schools across Pakistan do not have toilet facilities for students. In Sindh, 43% of primary schools do not have this facility and 25% of middle and seven per cent of high schools also do not have toilet facility. Similarly, there is regional discrepancy in terms of supply of electricity to schools across Pakistan. While Punjab and Federal Capital, Islamabad have managed to provide electricity to all primary schools, the figures are lower in other provinces. Only 15% schools in Baluchistan have access to electricity and the figure is 21% for Azad Jammu and Kashmir (AJK), 38% for Sindh, and 44% for Gilgit-Baltistan.[21] Such issue discourages the girls students particularly, majority of whom are already not going to schools, to attend schools in culturally conservative rural areas in Pakistan (Fig. 3.1).

In the second phase of CPEC, with the emphasis upon socio-economic development projects, there is an emphasis on improving education infrastructure in Pakistan. The CPEC's Joint Working Group (JWG) on socio-economic development was aimed to identify and ensure the implementation of pilot projects in education through setting up smart schools and knowledge sharing in faculty development programs and make efforts to equip youth with vocational training and improve high education resources.[22] Within this context, 18 universities from China and Pakistan established the CPEC Consortium of Universities in 2017. Later on, the number of participating universities increased to 110. The aim of the consortium was to promote academic exchanges for the

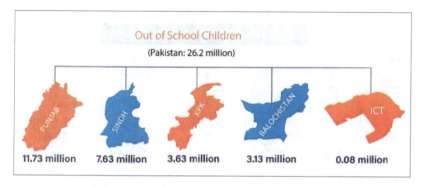

Fig. 3.1 Out of School Children in Pakistan (*Source* Kashif Abbasi, "Government Turns its Back on Education", *Dawn*, January 23, 2024, https://www.dawn.com/news/1807937)

high-quality development of CPEC. Major areas under the consortium included the establishment of China study centers at various universities across Pakistan, joint research projects, language training and talent cultivation, cultural activities and holding joint conferences, workshops and exhibitions.[23]

SDG 8 in Pakistan

The aim of SDG 8 is to foster sustained, inclusive and sustainable economic growth, full and productive employment and decent work for all in order to improve the overall quality of life.[24] Pakistan has placed this goal in Tier 1 due to its significance and impact on the lives of people. However, the objective of decent work and economic wellbeing under SDG 8 has slowed down with the slowing of GDP growth and plethora of economic problems faced by the country in recent years.[25] The economic growth submerged to 0.2% in 2023, down from 6.1% in 2022.[26]

According to the Macro Poverty Outlook report, prolonged and high inflation in food and energy prices, combined with a lack of substantial economic growth, could lead to social upheaval and negatively impact the well-being of disadvantaged households that have already seen their savings dwindle and incomes decline.[27] Pakistan is no exception in this regard. In the past several years Pakistan is faced with severe economic crisis and remains at the verge of economic meltdown due to massive external debt. The crisis was exacerbated by the derailment of the USD 6.5 billion International Monetary Fund (IMF) program that Pakistan entered in 2019. IMF was not satisfied with Pakistan's ability to arrange for funds to meet external financing requirements and it also doubted its ability to reform the system.[28]

In terms of Pakistan's performance in SDG 8, one indicator is the ratio of employment especially among youth. More than 60% population of Pakistan comprises of youth and a third of the total youth population remained out of educational institutions and subsequently unemployable.[29] During 2022, the unemployment rate in the country climbed to 4.2%.[30] The situation further got worst with the floods of 2022 that resulted in the massive destruction of infrastructure and loss of agrarian land and live stock hence affecting negatively the economic well being of communities living in the flood hit areas of Sindh and Punjab provinces. The floods submerged 1/3 of the country and affected 33 million people, causing damage of approximately USD 14.9 billion. A total of 4.3 million workers across all provinces have been affected, with varied income losses due to severity and duration of the impact.[31]

The Covid-19 pandemic also slowed down economic activity that resulted in loss of business and economic opportunities for communities at large. According to a report of the International Labor Organization (ILO), the global slowdown amid the Covid-19 pandemic caused a loss of 8.8% of global working hours in 2020 which is equivalent to 255 million full-time jobs. Pakistan is no exception in this regard, with projected Covid-19-triggered job losses of around 20 million.[32] The CPEC project has a positive impact on the SDG 8 especially in the context of job creation, where it has provided approximately 200,000 employment opportunities for local population in Pakistan.

Pakistan requires a multi-dimensional and people-sensitive approach to achieve the Millenium goals to ensure a more sustainable, inclusive, and prosperous future for all its citizens. Synchronization of CPEC with SDGs can lessen the burden on Pakistan's weak economy, where at times it gets difficult to focus on socio-economic development for the betterment of people while dealing with major issues such as handling inflation and debt restructuring.

Notes

1. "The 17 Goals," The Department of Economic and Social Affairs, *United Nations Organization*, https://sdgs.un.org/goals.
2. Iftikhar Ahmed, "SDGs & Pakistan: Navigating Challenges for Inclusive Growth," *The Express Tribune*, January 4, 2024, https://tribune.com.pk/story/2454181/sdgs-pakistan-navigating-challenges-for-inclusive-growth.
3. For further details, see National Initiative for Sustainable Development Goals, https://www.sdgpakistan.pk/web/sdgs.
4. "Rankings," Sustainable Development Report, https://dashboards.sdgindex.org/rankings.
5. Federal SDGs Support Unit, Ministry of Planning and Development, "Pakistan: SDGs Status Report 2021," 2021, https://dashboards.sdgindex.org/static/profiles/pdfs/SDR-2022-pakistan.pdf.
6. "Uniting Partners to Accelerate Pakistan's Progress Towards Health Related Sustainable Development Goals," *WHO*, December 2022, https://www.who.int/news-room/feature-stories/detail/uniting-partners-accelerate-pakistan-progress-health-sustainable-development-goals.
7. Salman J. Khan, Mohammad Asif, Sadia Aslam, Wahab J. Khan and Syed A. Hamza, "Pakistan's Healthcare System: A Review of Major Challenges and the First Comprehensive Universal Health Coverage Initiative," *Cureus* 4, no. 15 (2023): https://www.ncbi.nlm.nih.gov/pmc/articles/PMC10548490/.
8. Salman J. Khan, Mohammad Asif, Sadia Aslam, Wahab J. Khan and Syed A. Hamza, "Pakistan's Healthcare System: A Review of Major Challenges and the First Comprehensive Universal Health Coverage Initiative," *Cureus* 4, no. 15 (2023): https://www.ncbi.nlm.nih.gov/pmc/articles/PMC10548490/.
9. Sadia Sulaiman, "What CPEC Can Do for Our Health Sector?," *The Express Tribune*, August 18, 2022, https://tribune.com.pk/story/2371669/what-cpec-can-do-for-our-health-sector.
10. "Pakistan-China Friendship Hospital to be Opened Today," *CPEC*, December 4, 2023, https://cpecinfo.com/pak-china-friendship-hospital-to-be-opened-today/.
11. Kalbe Ali, "Karot Project Provides Social Uplift Opportunities to Locals," *Dawn*, June 20, 2023.

12. Muhammad Shahbaz, "China-Pakistan Health Corridor on Bilateral Health Care," *China Daily*, November 7, 2023, https://global.chinadaily.com.cn/a/202311/07/WS65499a57a31090682a5eccfb.html.
13. Madiha Arsalan Haneef, "Plight of Out of School Children," *The Friday Times*, January 29, 2024, https://thefridaytimes.com/09-Jan-2024/plight-of-the-out-of-school-children.
14. Zaigham Naqvi, "Number of Out of School Children Rises Sharply," *The Express Tribune*, January 22, 2024, https://tribune.com.pk/story/2454001/number-of-out-of-school-children-rises-sharply.
15. "Pakistan: SDGs Status Report 2021."
16. Zaigham Naqvi, "Number of Out of School Children Rises Sharply," *The Express Tribune*, January 22, 2024, https://tribune.com.pk/story/2454001/number-of-out-of-school-children-rises-sharply; Also see Kashif Abbasi, "Despite Lofty Claims, Out of School Children Soar to 28 Million," *Dawn*, October 17, 2023, https://www.dawn.com/news/1781436.
17. Muhammad Asad, "Out of School Children Need Urgent Attention," *The Express Tribune*, February 28, 2024, https://tribune.com.pk/story/2457797/out-of-school-children-need-urgent-attention.
18. Kashif Abbasi, "Government Turns Its Back on Education Sector," *Dawn*, January 23, 2024, https://www.dawn.com/news/1807937.
19. "Pakistan Yet to Prioritise Education Budgeting as Per SDG 4," *The News*, October 9, 2021, https://www.thenews.com.pk/print/898897-pakistan-yet-to-prioritise-education-budgeting-as-per-sdg-4.
20. Ahmad Ahmadani, "Education Sector Receives Marginal Budget Boost for 2023–24," *Profit*, June 9, 2023, https://profit.pakistantoday.com.pk/2023/06/09/education-sector-receives-marginal-budget-boost-for-2023-24/. For more details on budget cuts in education sector please see: Tahir Amin, "1.5 pc Dip: Education Gets Rs 90.556 bn," The Business Recorder, June 11, 2022, https://www.brecorder.com/news/40179416.
21. Kashif Abbasi, "Government Turns Its Back on Education Sector," *Dawn*, January 23, 2024, https://www.dawn.com/news/1807937.

22. Zeenat Erum, "A Study of the Impact of CPEC on Educational Development in Gwadar," *Journal of Social Sciences and Media Studies* 4, no. 01 (2020): (18–25) 20.
23. "Educational Cooperation Between Pakistan, China Promotes High Quality CPEC Development, Says Expert," *Xinhua*, December 28, 2022, http://english.scio.gov.cn/m/beltandroad/2022-12/28/content_85030011.htm.
24. "Pakistan's Development on Sustainable Development Goal 8: Decent Work and Economic Growth," *Imarat Institute of Public Policy*, 2021, https://iips.com.pk/pakistans-progress-on-sustainable-development-goal-8-decent-work-and-economic-growth/.
25. Federal SDGs Support Unit, Ministry of Planning and Development, "Pakistan: SDGs Status Report 2021," 2021, https://dashboards.sdgindex.org/static/profiles/pdfs/SDR-2022-pakistan.pdf.
26. Ibid.
27. "Poverty Surges Across Pakistan with Food, Energy Prices Spike: World Bank," *Business Standard*, October 21, 2023, https://www.business-standard.com/world-news/poverty-surges-across-pakistan-with-food-energy-prices-spike-world-bank-123102100786_1.html.
28. Shahbaz Rana, "Pakistan's Existential Economic Crisis," Analysis by USIP, April 2023, https://www.usip.org/publications/2023/04/pakistans-existential-economic-crisis.
29. Ibid.
30. Ibid.
31. "Pakistan's Floods 2022: Post Disaster Need Assessment," International Labour Organization, November 2022, https://www.ilo.org/global/topics/employment-promotion/recovery-and-reconstruction/WCMS_862500/lang--en/index.htm.
32. Karim Khan, "SDG-8 and Post-Covid Pakistan," The Express Tribune, July 13, 2021, https://tribune.com.pk/story/2310181/sdg-8-and-post-covid-pakistan.

CHAPTER 4

CPEC and the Delivery of Public Goods in Azad Jammu and Kashmir

Abstract This chapter examines the impact of the Kohala Hydropower Project on local communities. However, it starts with an analysis of the impact that the Neelum Jhelum Hydroelectric Project (NJHP), which is not part of CPEC but one of the biggest Chinese initiatives in Pakistan in the energy sector. The study finds resentment among the local communities towards Kohala Hydropower Project due to the associated environmental and economic challenges. The locals were not convinced of the benefits of NJHP, hence apprehensive of the Kohala Hydropower project with minimum possible impact on SDGs 3, 4 and 8.

Keywords Azad Jammu and Kashmir · CPEC · Kohala Hydropower Project · Neelum Jhelum Hydroelectric Project (NJHP) · Environment

INTRODUCTION

Azad Jammu and Kashmir (AJK), a self-governing administrative unit in Pakistan, has a population of 4.11 million with 88% of the population residing in rural areas that can be categorized as underdeveloped.[1] AJK has a literacy rate of 77% and unemployment ratio is 10.3%. The region plays significant role in economy of Pakistan, since it has three major rivers, the Neelum, the Jehlum and the Poonch, and numerous other

© The Author(s), under exclusive license to Springer Nature Switzerland AG 2024
S. Sulaiman, *The CPEC and SDGs in Pakistan*,
https://doi.org/10.1007/978-3-031-65579-1_4

streams. These water resources are crucial for water resources and generation of hydropower in Pakistan. Major sources of income in the region include subsistence agriculture, livestock rearing, tourism, small/cottage industry hydropower, services and Government jobs.[2]

The AJK Government is fully committed to implementing the Sustainable Development Goals (SDGs). Its Planning and Development Department (P&DD) is playing a key role in this by ensuring coordination among government and non-government stakeholders for the smooth and successful attainment of these goals. Within this context, Vision 2025 or the 12th Five-Year Plan was linked with the SDGs to ensure proper and continuous implementation of the 2030 Agenda.[3] However, these efforts are not without challenges where the key challenge is lack of coordination among various stakeholders leading towards murky goals with shaky roadmaps.

As far as the China-Pakistan Economic Corridor (CPEC) is concerned, it has rolled out in AJK at a slower pace comparatively than the rest of the country, leading to a lack of clarity about the viability and impact of these projects. For AJK, the Kohala and Karot hydropower projects, the Mirpur Special Economic Zone, and the Mansehra-Muzaffarabad-Mirpur-Mangla Expressway project under the CPEC have been approved. This chapter examines the impact of the Kohala Hydropower Project on local communities. However, as explained earlier, it starts with an analysis of the impact that the Neelum Jhelum Hydroelectric Project (NJHP) has had on the delivery of SDGs 3, 4, and 8 in the communities affected by the project.

THE NEELUM-JHELUM HYDROELECTRIC PROJECT

While the NJHP predates the CPEC, it set the stage for Pakistan-China cooperation in big infrastructure projects in many ways. The project involved two rivers, Neelum and Jhelum, which flow through Muzaffarabad, AJK's capital city. A consortium consisting of China Gezhouba Group Co. Ltd. (CGGC) and China Machinery Engineering Corp was awarded the 21-billion-yuan contract in 2008. The project mandated constructing a dam to divert the Neelum river, a waterway system consisting of 68-kilometer-long tunnels as well as an underground powerhouse on the Jhelum river.[4]

Upon completion, the project promised to provide 969 megawatts of electricity to the national grid and 8000 jobs for locals and ensure that tourism and other activities in the region were not disrupted. The glacier-fed rivers resulted in pleasant weather for the region, which made it a major tourist attraction. The rivers also served as a natural waste management system for the city's untreated sewage. While Pakistan's Water and Power Development Authority (WAPDA) was primarily responsible for running the project, the Chinese consortium was tasked with building sewage treatment plants and three artificial lakes, as well as ensuring that the rivers always retained necessary water levels to keep the city cool. However, less attention was paid to these requirements, leading to environmental concerns as well as a significant impact on the lives and livelihoods of residents.[5]

Infrastructure

A devastating earthquake affected much of the infrastructure facilities in Muzaffarabad, the site of the project, in 2005. While massive rebuilding has been carried on since then, the city still lacks facilities for the delivery of public goods, including schools and health facilities.[6] The WAPDA has constructed a girls' high school, a bridge, and a road in the area of the project.[7] However, while roads were built to ease the delivery of construction materials to the project location, no attempts have been made to extend these roads to connect schools or health centers with residential areas. Moreover, the shortage of water as a result of the NJHP has adversely affected educational facilities. Some schools even remained closed for parts of the year because of the unavailability of water in the school facilities.[8]

The diversion of rivers and changes in the waste management mechanism is believed to have contributed to an increase in water-borne and insect-borne diseases, such as hepatitis, malaria, and typhoid.[9] However, the status of health infrastructure remains vastly inadequate. A field hospital was set up as part of the project, which is believed to have catered to those living close to it.[10] No change in health infrastructure was reported beyond this one instance. None of the roads built for the NJHP connected to the already existing health facilities in Muzaffarabad city.[11]

The impact of the project on the environment has been a significant concern through the years. However, despite the intervention of the AJK High Court, the WAPDA did not approach the provincial authorities for an agreement to work together on environmental impact mitigation. In fact, the project was completed long after the conditional no objection certificate given to the agencies expired.[12] Natural water springs serving the community were disturbed by the project, and despite proposals to set up new water supply facilities, nothing was done.[13] As a result, once-existing water channels dried out due to lack of rain, and little water was available for agriculture and livestock. The growth of wheat, rice, apples, pears, and vegetables suffered after the diversion of the Neelum river.[14] Tourism, the other major income generator, was affected as the city no longer had the pleasant weather that used to bring in tourists. The damage to economic activity, including agriculture and tourism, has forced many to migrate out of the area for better opportunities.[15]

Claims About the Project, and the Reality

Politicians from ruling parties, whether at the federal level or in AJK, have usually supported the project, claiming that it would lead to prosperity in the region. In most instances, the statements avoid addressing specific issues, sticking to generic forward-looking claims, such as that the NJHP will help tackle electricity shortfall or generate jobs in the region. The then prime minister Nawaz Sharif claimed in 2016 that the project would produce cheap and affordable electricity and contribute to the local economy.[16] Government officials have also claimed that the companies in charge of the project were required to address the needs of the local population under a community investment program. This reportedly includes the construction of roads, schools, and other facilities.[17]

However, locals say that even after the completion of the project, power cuts persist in Muzaffarabad, affecting business.[18] Unemployment is a major concern—unemployment rates in AJK touched 11% in 2017–2018, almost double the national average of 5.9%.[19] Through the years, locals have continued to protest against the appointment of non-locals in the project.[20] According to them, locals were only employed as laborers in the project, while the better jobs went to people from Punjab and KP, and the technical positions were filled by the Chinese.[21] As a local explained, jobs for locals were "a mere drop in the ocean."[22]

Response from Citizens and Civil Society

The NJHP is significant in the way public opinion has coalesced into popular movements, although at a small scale, attempting to hold authorities responsible. Civil society members and common citizens were explicit in their opinion that the opacity in the planning and operation of the project had been the most significant problem from the outset. In the aftermath of the construction of the NJHP, the local people initiated a movement called "Save the Rivers" to attract the attention of the governments of AJK and Pakistan toward the economic and environmental impact of the project.[23] They claimed that this made economic activity difficult, leading to instances of migration and displacement.[24] They said that they were never clear on what percentage of electricity generated from the project would benefit the local population.[25] The authorities were noncommittal about their policies for the mitigation of environmental impact.

Civil society leaders have also alleged irregularities in the process involving land acquisition and other procedures related to the project.[26] This includes lack of adherence to rules of procurement, absence of external auditing of project cost, and allegations of kickbacks.[27] These have increased public grievances, leading to the mobilization of civil society activists and the organization of protests.[28] These were done with the primary objective of pointing out the degradation in the quality of life of the locals and asking for remediation. However, when protests persisted over time, the government responded by arresting activists and dismantling sit-in camps.[29]

Locals believe that conditions are made worse by a lopsided system that works against local interests. They claim that AJK receives a minuscule share of the revenue from the sale of electricity, lower than what other regions of the country receive.[30] They also believe that they are discriminated against by the WAPDA. Multiple respondents recounted instances of employees being falsely promised permanent government jobs after a few years as contractual workers.[31]

Kohala Hydropower Project

The 1124-megawatt Kohala Hydropower Project (KHP) is being constructed on the Jhelum river close to Muzaffarabad. The agreement was signed in 2020, and the project is expected to be completed in

2027.[32] This USD 2.4 billion project will be constructed by China's Three Gorges South Asia Investment Ltd. (CSAIL) and is believed to be one of the largest investments in the country in a single project. According to CPEC authorities, the project will be operational for a hundred years and will be handed over to the AJK government after thirty years, allowing the AJK government to earn taxes on electricity produced from the project.[33]

Authorities claim that the project will produce five billion units of green electricity for consumers across the country.[34] They have pegged the number of jobs for the local community from the project at around 10,000. Locals, however, are less than convinced by these claims, especially after their experience with the NJHP. Civil society leaders claim that their concerns, which are similar to those raised during the NJHP, have been again met with equivocation and vague promises, which makes them suspicious.[35]

Infrastructure

Kohala is close to Muzaffarabad and is dependent on the city for economic opportunities as well as education and health infrastructure, with minimum facilities available locally.[36] Along with Muzaffarabad, it suffered from a lack of adequate delivery of public goods after the 2005 earthquake. As in the case of the NJHP, the company in charge of the project is required to have a community investment program for the KHP to fulfill the needs of the community. The program involves plans to construct mother-child health centers and a hospital for the community. There are also plans to improve communication infrastructure in the area to help improve economic and other opportunities.[37] The program has promised to help develop a plan to mitigate the effect of the project on the environment.

CSAIL's community investment program includes plans to construct schools and technical institutions and award scholarships under various exchange programs with Chinese organizations.[38] To build confidence in the community and to demonstrate commitment, the company in charge of the project has already facilitated scholarships for around 300 local students.[39] Separately, twenty-two students from those displaced by the project have been given scholarships for technical education in China.[40]

Claims About the Project, and the Reality

Despite these initial steps, the question of compensation for land for the project continues to be a sticking point. Residents feel that there is an absence of a consistent policy in determining the sum to be paid. The government agreed to pay PKR 1,500,000 for about 500 square meters of land. However, once the locals discovered that people in nearby projects had been compensated at a higher rate, they started to refuse to surrender their land and approach courts of law. Some others report having surrendered their land on which project work has begun, even though they have not been compensated.[41]

Referring to the NJHP, locals connected the compensation to environmental impact, arguing that compensation should reflect not only the cost of land but also that of environmental consequences.[42] The local press has also highlighted this aspect, drawing comparisons between the two projects.[43] Some of the affected have demanded compensation to the tune of PKR 5,000,000 per 500 square meters of land.[44] As a result, even as work on the project is on, land acquisition has been taking place in fits and starts.[45]

The government, however, has refuted this narrative, emphasizing the involvement of the federal Environment Protection Agency (EPA), which, they say, makes the Kohala project vastly different from the NJHP. They say that the EPA has been involved in the early stages of the KHP so that they can ensure that issues like the supply of water for agriculture and other activities are addressed.[46] Some local businessmen associated with the project have also sided with the government, claiming that safeguards have been built into the project in the form of a no-objection certificate for the project getting canceled if the concerns of the people are not met.[47] Additionally, the government, including the prime minister, has claimed that the project will ensure employment for the youth of AJK.[48]

Response from Citizens and Civil Society

Three issues—compensation, potential employment opportunities, and mitigation of environmental impact—have dominated the discourse on the ground regarding this project. There have already been reports of some people suffering due to the acquisition of cultivable land without resolution of the compensation issue.[49] Reports suggest that thousands more may be affected unless the project accounts for the rehabilitation of the local population.[50] Educated young people in Kohala expect to be hired for the project and have demanded that they be given priority.[51] According to some residents, once the project is operational, the KHP workers and their families will increase opportunities for local businesses catering to daily requirements.[52] Locals also expect that the influx of these people will lead to an overall upliftment of the community, including better connectivity and improved facilities for education and health.[53]

There is considerable support among locals for investment in social infrastructure as planned in the community investment program. Some believe that if the initiatives planned are executed adequately, the delivery of public goods in the region will be substantially improved. However, media reports suggest disbelief among the people about the promises.[54] Their experience with the NJHP has alerted citizens about the risks to water sources that the community depends on. The NJHP had reduced water flow in the Neelum river downstream of the dam site in Nauseri, impacting local communities. The KHP too envisages a diversion in the Jhelum river, against which locals have protested.[55] Additionally, assessment reports for the KHP have indicated potential risks to areas between Saran and Kohala due to the absence of alternative water sources as well as the risk of the river bed drying out after the creation of the dam.[56] A charter of demands has now been constituted by local organizations, along with a movement to save the river, aimed at building awareness about these issues and ensuring mobilization in the community.[57]

Finally, locals have questioned the propriety of the way the project was handed over to CSAIL. They claim that the process of awarding the contract was not transparent, including the absence of an open tendering process and the lack of information about the parameters that were examined while making the decision.[58] This lack of clarity has led to concerns that as in the case of the NJHP, the electricity generated from the KHP will also be distributed to the rest of the country with minimum benefits to AJK.[59]

An analysis of the existing issues in AJK indicates that the experience with NJHP and the active participation by the civil society has played an active role in the way the KHP has been perceived by the local people. Though the NJHP has been outside the ambit of the CPEC, experiences of inadequate compensation, environmental degradation (affecting economic opportunities), and lack of transparency from the project have led to more critical questions being asked in the case of the KHP. This has resulted in a more robust community investment program being developed. However, there is still a significant lack of clarity on ways in which the KHP plans to improve the state of the community especially with reference to SDG 3, 4 and 8. While some promises about better education and health facilities have been made, they are not central to the plan for the project. Comments from officials and elected representatives have focused more on creating employment opportunities as a crucial aspect of the project.

Table 4.1 summarizes the situation of delivery of public goods in AJK against each indicator used in the Theoretical Framework. It finds out that the existing health and education infrastructure requires upgradation and economic well-being is the key promise and consideration by the government and people both. However, the experience of the local communities with NJHP gave rise to an active civil society who played a key role in raising awareness regarding environmental impacts of the projects.

Table 4.1 Delivery of Public Goods in AJK

Indicator	NJHP	KHP
Existing Infrastructure	SDG 3: Preliminary SDG 4: Preliminary SDG 8: Preliminary	SDG 3: Preliminary SDG 4: Preliminary SDG 8: Preliminary
Access to Existing Infrastructure	SDG 3: Preliminary SDG 4: Preliminary SDG 8: Preliminary	SDG 3: Preliminary SDG 4: Preliminary SDG 8: Preliminary
Projection of Projects	As a Source of better economic opportunities	As a Source of better socio-economic options
Actual Impact	SDG 3: Nil SDG 4: Nil SDG 8: Slight improvement in local employment	SDG 3: To be Determined SDG 4: To be Determined SDG 8: To be Determined
Citizens' Response	SDG 3: No Demand SDG 4: Technical Education demanded SDG 8: Local jobs demanded	SDG 3: Demand for better health infrastructure SDG 4: Technical Education demanded SDG 8: Local jobs demanded
Miscellaneous	Environmental Concerns played a key role in delivery of public goods	Environmental Concerns played a key role in delivery of public goods Active role of Civil Society in raising awareness

Notes

1. Azad Jammu and Kashmir Official Portal, accessed February 17, 2022, https://www.ajk.gov.pk/ajk-at-a-glance.
2. Nihan Rafique and Syed Ali Husnain Gillani, "Implementation of Sustainable Development Goals in AJ&K and the Way Forward," Report by Planning and Development Department, Azad Government of the State of Jammu and Kashmir, September 2020, https://pndajk.gov.pk/uploadfiles/downloads/Implementation%20of%20SDGs%20in%20AJK%20and%20Way%20Forward%20Final%20Sep%202020.pdf.
3. Ibid.
4. "Pakistan Neelum-Jhelum Project to Start Operation: Chinese Contractor," *Xinhuanet*, April 12, 2018, http://www.xinhuanet.com/english/2018-04/12/c_137106695.htm.
5. Interview with Stakeholder F2, December 2020.
6. Tariq Naqash, "16 Years Since Quake, Fate of 1730 Projects in AJK Remains Uncertain," *Dawn*, October 9, 2021, https://www.dawn.com/news/1650888.
7. Interview with Stakeholder E2, December 2020; Interview with Stakeholder F2, December 2020.
8. Interview with Stakeholder F1, December 2020.
9. Roshan Mughal, "Pakistani Kashmir Residents Fear Power Project Will Destroy Economy, Livelihood," Voice of America, August 25, 2020, https://www.voanews.com/south-central-asia/pakistani-kashmir-residents-fear-power-project-will-destroy-economy-livelihood.
10. Interview with Stakeholder H1, December 2020.
11. Interview with Stakeholder F2, December 2020.
12. Ibid.
13. Ibid.
14. Interview with Stakeholder F1, December 2020.
15. Murtaza Ali Shah, "Protestors Demand Protection of Muzaffarabad Environment, Economy," *The News*, April 17, 2019, https://www.thenews.com.pk/print/459077-protesters-demand-protection-of-muzaffarabad-environment-economy.
16. "Nawaz Sharif Said That Government Is Determined to Complete Energy Projects on Time," *Daily Ausaf*, August 13, 2016; "Neelum-Jhelum Project Labourers Are Waiting for Their Salary,

Construction Company Started Firing Labourers," *Daily Ausaf*, November 29, 2017.
17. Interview with Stakeholder C1, December 2020.
18. Interview with Stakeholder D13, July 2021; Interview with Stakeholder A10, July 2021.
19. Mubarak Zeb Khan, "AJK's Employment Rate Put at 10.3pc in 2017–18," *Dawn*, March 3, 2019, https://www.dawn.com/news/1467289.
20. "Protest Erupts Against Neelum-Jhelum Hydropower Project in Pakistan-occupied Kashmir," *New Indian Express*, July 30, 2019, https://www.newindianexpress.com/world/2019/jul/30/protest-erupts-against-neelum-jhelum-hydropower-project-in-pakistan-occupied-kashmir-2011533.html; Anurakti Sharma, "China Puts Neelum-Jhelum Hydropower Project in PoK on Backburner as Bankrupt Pakistan Delays Payments," *Times Now World*, February 4, 2023, https://www.timesnownews.com/world/china-puts-neelum-jhelum-hydropower-project-in-pok-on-backburner-as-bankrupt-pakistan-delays-payments-article-97592863.
21. Interview with Stakeholder H2, December 2020.
22. Interview with Stakeholder E2, December 2020.
23. Murtaza Ali Shah, "Protestors Demand Protection of Muzaffarabad Environment, Economy," *The News*, April 17, 2019, https://www.thenews.com.pk/print/459077-protesters-demand-protection-of-muzaffarabad-environment-economy.
24. Interview with Stakeholder F1, December 2020; see also Manzoor Hussain Gillani v. Neelum–Jhelum HPP, AJK High Court (November 2019), https://ajkhighcourt.gok.pk/judgment_files/Neelum_Jehlum_Writ_No_1675-21018.pdf.
25. Interview with Stakeholder F2, December 2020.
26. Interview with Stakeholder E1, January 2020; Zahid Ali, "Neelum-Jhelum Hydroelectric Project: An Ongoing Saga of Corruption and Financial Irregularities," *Sujag*, accessed May 30, 2023, https://loksujag.com/story/neelum-jhelum-hydropower-project-eng.
27. "ECNEC Approves Neelum-Jhelum Project at Rs507b Cost," *The Express Tribune*, May 23, 2018, https://tribune.com.pk/story/1716539/ecnec-approves-neelum-jhelum-project-rs507b-cost; "Neelum Jhelum Project: 'Hasty Project Launch Caused

Huge Losses'," *The Express Tribune*, December 9, 2015, https://tribune.com.pk/story/1007249/neelum-jhelum-project-hasty-project-launch-caused-huge-losses.
28. Interview with Stakeholder F2, December 2020; "Muzaffarabad Citizens Protest Neelum Jhelum Power Project," *Dawn*, September 17, 2018, https://www.dawn.com/news/1433321; see also Tariq Naqash, "PPP Calls on WAPDA, Government to Address Concerns Regarding Neelum Jhelum Project," *Dawn*, October 29, 2017, https://www.dawn.com/news/1367049.
29. Tariq Naqash, "Police Action Against Civil Society Alliance in Muzaffarabad Condemned," *Dawn*, June 18, 2019, https://www.dawn.com/news/1488819.
30. Interview with Stakeholder E2, December 2020.
31. Maham Tahir, "Neelm Jhelum Hydro Power Employees Warn to Strike," *Graana* (blog), September 15, 2019, https://www.graana.com/blog/neelum-jhelum-hydro-power-project-employees-warn-to-strike/.
32. CPEC Official Website, https://cpec.gov.pk/project-details/23.
33. Mughal, "Pakistani Kashmir Residents Fear Power Project Will Destroy Economy, Livelihood."
34. "Four Hydro Power Projects to Attract $7.7b Investment," *The Nation*, May 4, 2021, https://nation.com.pk/04-May-2021/four-hydro-power-projects-to-attract-dollar-7-7b-investment.
35. Interview with Stakeholder F2, December 2020; see also Mughal, "Pakistani Kashmir Residents Fear Power Will Destroy Economy, Livelihood."
36. Interview with Stakeholder A2, December 2020.
37. "Kohala Hydropower Plant," Environmental Protection Agency of Government of Azad Jammu and Kashmir, December 22, 2016, http://www.epaajk.gok.pk/uploadfiles/downloads/Construction%20of%201124%20MW%20kohala%20hydropower%20project(KHPP).pdf.
38. "Kohala Hydropower Plant," December 22, 2016.
39. Interview with Stakeholder D13, July 2021.
40. Interview with Stakeholder E3, January 2021.
41. Interview with Stakeholder E4, January 2020; Interview with Stakeholder E3, January 2021.
42. Interview with Stakeholder H1, December 2020.

43. Zafar Bhutta, "Kohala Hydropower Project Hits Snags," *The Express Tribune*, February 4, 2020, https://tribune.com.pk/story/2149706/kohala-hydropower-project-hits-snags.
44. "Kohala Hydropower Plant," December 22, 2016.
45. Interview with Stakeholder E4, January 2020; Mushtaq Ghumman, "Land Issue of Kohala HPP: C-SAIL Seeks Support of PPIB," *Business Recorder*, December 14, 2022, https://www.brecorder.com/news/40214398; Zafar Bhutta, "Kohala Hydropower Project Hits Snags," *Express Tribune*, February 4, 2020, https://tribune.com.pk/story/2149706/kohala-hydropower-project-hits-snags.
46. Interview with Stakeholder C1, December 2020.
47. Interview with Stakeholder B1, December 2020.
48. "$2.4 Billion Kohala Power Project Signing Ceremony Held," *The Express Tribune*, June 26, 2020, https://tribune.com.pk/story/2250372/2-4b-kohala-power-project-signing-ceremony-held.
49. Interview with Stakeholder E4, January 2021.
50. "Kohala Power Project Can Affect Thousand People: City Reporter," *Daily Ausaf*, October 19, 2016.
51. Interview with Stakeholder E1, January 2021.
52. Interview with Stakeholder C1, December 2020.
53. Interview with Stakeholder B1, December 2020; Interview with Stakeholder C1, December 2020.
54. Tariq Naqash, "AJK Government Sets Conditions for Kohala Power Project," *Dawn*, July 15, 2019, https://www.dawn.com/news/1494144.
55. Ibid.
56. Interview with Stakeholder F2, December 2020.
57. Interview with Stakeholder E2, December 2020; Interview with Stakeholder E3, January 2020; Interview with Stakeholder H1, December 2020.
58. Interview with Stakeholder F2, December 2020.
59. Interview with Stakeholder A10, July 2021.

CHAPTER 5

CPEC and the Delivery of Public Goods in Khyber Pakhtunkhwa

Abstract In this chapter, the effect of two ongoing CPEC projects in Khyber Pakhtunkhwa (KP) province—the Rashakai Special Economic Zone (RSEZ) and the Peshawar–Dera Ismail (D.I.) Khan Motorway—on the lives of the local communities is examined. Being a conflict-affected region with 80% of the population living in rural areas, there are high expectations among the locals about the impact of CPEC changing their lives for the better. The overall focus of CPEC at this point of time is on SDG8 and with little focus on SDG 3 and 4.

Keywords Khyber Pakhtunkhwa (KP) · CPEC · SDGs · Rashakai Special Economic Zone (RSEZ) · Peshawar–Dera Ismail (D.I.) Khan Motorway · Rural Pakistan

Introduction

As in Azad Jammu and Kashmir (AJK), the majority of the population in Khyber Pakhtunkhwa (KP), as much as 82%, lives in rural areas.[1] Urban centers are limited to Peshawar, the capital of the province, and its surrounding areas. The province suffers from inadequate delivery of health and education facilities and offers few economic opportunities, which are instead primarily concentrated in the major cities of

© The Author(s), under exclusive license to Springer Nature Switzerland AG 2024
S. Sulaiman, *The CPEC and SDGs in Pakistan*,
https://doi.org/10.1007/978-3-031-65579-1_5

the province. To attain equitable and sustainable economic development goals, the Government of KP has developed its own Sustainable Development Strategy (2019–2023), Provincial SDGs Framework (2019–2030) and Tribal Decade Strategy.[2] All of these policies provide a framework to achieve SDGs in the KP and the adjacent Newly Merged Tribal Districts (NMDs) on border with Afghanistan.

However, the implementation of these policies is not without challenges as the province has witnessed low-intensity conflict in the post-9/11 scenario which still affects the region. For example, education sector suffered immense loses due to destruction of education infrastructure and banning the girls form going to school. As a result of that conflict, almost 3.5 million people were internally displaced and they lost their livelihood. The uncertain security situation also hampered the pace of China-Pakistan Economic Corridor (CPEC) projects in the province. Most of the projects witnessed delay in the initiation and some still await final approval.

KP along with Baluchistan have always blamed Punjab for a major share in the CPEC while ignoring these smaller provinces. For example, Out of the USD 21 billion worth of "priority energy projects", there was only one project in KP (worth USD 1.8 billion) and two in Baluchistan (worth USD 1.3 billion), accounting for 8.5% and six percent, respectively, of the total investment categorized as "priority".[3]

According to official sources recently an MoU was signed between Ministry of Planning, Development and Reform, Pakistan and China International Development Agency on implementation of the Projects under Joint Working Group (JWG) of CPEC on Socio-Economic Development. In this regard, projects in the field of agriculture, education, medical treatment, poverty alleviation, water supply and vocational training were given a priority and total 44 projects were proposed in which 27 are Priority Projects and 17 are Fast Track Projects.[4]

In this chapter, the effect of two ongoing projects—the Rashakai Special Economic Zone (RSEZ) and the Peshawar–Dera Ismail (D.I.) Khan Motorway—on the lives of the local communities is examined.

Rashakai Special Economic Zone

The Rashakai Special Economic Zone, proposed as a priority project among CPEC's special economic zones, is being developed at the cost of USD 242 million, half of which is expected to come as foreign direct investment in the country. The agreement for the project, spread over

1000 acres about 70 kilometers from Peshawar, was signed in April 2019.[5] The SEZ is planned to be developed in the public-private partnership model by KP Economic Zone Development and Management Company (KPEZDMC) in collaboration with China Road & Bridge Corporation (CRBC).[6]

The project is planned in three phases, each focusing on establishing a particular set of industries, from textile to steel and heavy machinery to information technology (see Table 5.1). The first phase of the Project was completed in early 2023. The RSEZ is approximately 80 km and 60 km away from the New Islamabad International Airport and Bacha Khan International Airport, Peshawar while ML1 (Peshawar-Karachi) Railway project would connect it with the main cities such as Islamabad, Lahore and Karachi.[7] It will be linked by highway and rail to Gwadar Port to the south, Xinjiang via the Karakoram Highway to the north, and Afghanistan, Iran, Tajikistan, and other Central Asian nations to the west, thereby emerging as an important transit point for trade between Pakistan, Afghanistan, North-West China, Central Asia, and the markets in the Arabian Gulf. Former Prime Minister of Pakistan, Imran Khan described the RSEZ as an opportunity for the domestic economy to learn from China.[8] The Chinese ambassador has highlighted the project as key to accelerating economic progress and creating jobs.[9] With the likelihood of manufacturing units and ancillary services establishing bases in the SEZ, locals expect the project to substantially improve the delivery of public goods for them. However, as in the case of projects in AJK, the primary issues in KP are a lack of centrality in health and education in the expected outcomes for the project and a lack of data backing the claims of economic opportunities arising from the project.

Infrastructure

The RSEZ's closeness to Peshawar has traditionally addressed the requirement for higher education and specialized healthcare. The M1 motorway, which was opened for operation in 2007, has allowed locals to access nearby urban centers with greater ease. Locals agree that the road infrastructure, including the recently constructed Swat motorway, adequately addresses the requirements for accessing SDG 3 and SDG 4 at present.[10] Additionally, nearby urban centers, such as Mardan and Nowshera, provide additional support in the form of two medical colleges and their respective teaching hospitals.[11]

Table 5.1 Development Phases of Rashakai Special Economic Zone

S. No.	RSEZ development phases	Targets
1.	Phase One	• One hundred small factories • Industries of pharmaceutical, textile, food and beverage, homebuilding material, and electronic appliances
2	Phase Two	• Next batch of one hundred factories • Industries of steel, medicine, food, textiles, and light and heavy machinery parts
3	Phase Three	• Initiation of information technology city • Production of hardware, software, and other items of IT

However, the development of the Rashakai project is expected to attract additional people to the region, and the project does not seem to have concrete plans to address that as yet. There is no plan in place to audit existing facilities and develop additional ones to plug the existing gaps in service delivery. Emerging exigencies are also likely to include an inflow of Afghan refugees given that the project site is a little over 100 kilometers from land crossings between Pakistan and Afghanistan at Torkham.

Claims About the Project, and the Reality

In 2019, China's ambassador to Pakistan expressed an intention to build infrastructure including health facilities at the Torkham border to facilitate trade between Afghanistan and the RSEZ.[12] There is speculation that these facilities could be linked with the RSEZ or share some of the pressure that the facilities in Rashakai are likely to face. However, for now, the plan is limited to constructing a small hospital inside the SEZ to cater to the needs of the employees. As in other CPEC projects, residents will likely be able to access the facilities.[13] The KP government has said that it plans to develop a project called the CPEC City close to the RSEZ, which is expected to support the latter with an airport, technical training institutes, and universities.[14] However, currently, few details are available about the plan.

Officials associated with the RSEZ have claimed that three technical institutes in the surrounding districts of Mardan, Charsaddda, and Swabi will be set up to train those who will be employed in the RSEZ. The initial training will be provided by Chinese instructors, who will prepare potential employees according to the needs of the project.[15] The University of Technology under the KP government is also believed to have acquired additional land to set up a training facility for the RSEZ.[16] Beyond these training institutes, however, there is no plan to establish facilities catering to health and education.[17]

Much of the conversation about the development in Rashakai has revolved around the economic opportunities the projects under the RSEZ will bring, which are difficult to estimate as they swing wildly between official estimates and political claims. For instance, the estimate of jobs for 200,000 people has been widely reported. Even the former Prime Minister Imran Khan repeated the number while inaugurating the project, and it has since been repeated by other elected representatives and politicians.[18] Since then, the claims about potential job creation have increased, first to 250,000, and then to 300,000, with little clarity on when they will be available in a project that is estimated to be completed over phases till 2030.[19] The other major question involves the ratio of Chinese to Pakistani workers in the projects, which has been a point of discussion in other CPEC projects as well. The KPEZDMC authorities claim that, according to an agreement signed with the Chinese authorities, 80% of the jobs will go to Pakistanis, while the remaining roles will be fulfilled by Chinese experts.[20] Over time, local people will be trained to take up the roles being fulfilled by the Chinese.[21] Locals report that there has already been a push from the government toward learning Chinese as well as picking up technical skills to improve employability.[22]

A major concern for industries opting to set up units at the RSEZ has been a steady supply of electricity and gas. The KPEZDMC has claimed that the requirement of both has been accurately calculated and will be made available through federal authorities. Once electricity and gas reach the project, the CRBC will oversee the internal distribution and monitoring of the resources.[23] However, those that have opted to set up their units in the SEZ are not completely convinced that adequate arrangements have been made for the smooth functioning of units.[24]

Response from Citizens and Civil Society

The project has elicited mixed responses from the local community. On the one hand, in a region in dire need of better opportunities and facilities, the creation of a major project indicates the possibility of a better life. At the same time, the lack of information and contradictory statements have been met with skepticism. Locals have been impatient with the slow pace of development, claiming that, as of now, the project is merely a subject of speeches as locals have not benefited from the developments.[25] They have also questioned the lack of clarity on the kind of technological support that they may receive as part of the SEZ.

The policy over the acquisition of land has also emerged as an issue. Local landowners say that the process has been opaque and inconsistent, forcing them to protest and approach courts of law in certain cases. They believe that a lack of coordination between the Chinese agencies working on the project and the KP government is responsible for compensation issues.[26] There have also been concerns about whether all stakeholders are aware of their rights as residents and landowners and therefore able to ask for what is due to them.[27]

Farming and trading in cloth have been the traditional occupations in Nowshera and Rashakai.[28] With land acquisition picking up, many of the inhabitants are now reported to be without land required for their operations, affecting existing economic activity.[29] Traders and landowners awaiting compensation have asked for their kin to be employed in the RSEZ or for their businesses to be given priority accommodation in the SEZ.[30] Community leaders report that they are being asked by local youth for assistance in finding a job. They also report meeting government officials from federal and local authorities with the demand. However, while political promises have been made, there is little movement on the ground.[31] For now, only a few young men have been hired as security guards for the RSEZ. While the number of people appointed for CPEC security across Pakistan stands at more than 4500, no specific numbers for the Rashakai project are available.[32] Locals are concerned that in the absence of upskilling opportunities, positions for Pakistanis will be filled by people with better skills from other provinces like Punjab.[33] There are also questions about the exact roles that will be open to Pakistanis, with the apprehension that technically qualified roles and positions for experts will be open only to Chinese employees, considering their substantial investment in the project.[34]

In the absence of specific plans for the development of health or education facilities, the local community has pinned its hopes on the completion of the road infrastructure for the SEZ. Apart from better roads making it easier for them to reach Peshawar for better schools or hospitals, they expect such improvements to also bolster tourism.[35] Peshawar, Nowshera, Swabi, and Haripur are four major centers for hosting refugees in KP, which suggests that they need an updated healthcare system. The World Bank has recently pledged $200 million for the upgradation of health facilities in these areas.[36] However, as work on the RSEZ progresses, there will be additional pressure on healthcare, education, and economic systems in the region.

Peshawar–D.I. Khan Motorway

The Peshawar–D.I. Khan motorway is another key CPEC project in the province aimed at connecting some of the poorest and most underdeveloped parts of KP.[37] In October 2020, the China–Pakistan Joint Working Group (JWG) took up a proposal to construct multiple motorways, including a 399-kilometer-long one from Peshawar to Dera Ismail Khan, the second phase of the 182-kilometer-long Swat Expressway from Chakdara to Fatehpur, and the 30-kilometer-long Dir Expressway.[38] The Peshawar–D.I. Khan motorway was included among CPEC projects in September 2021 to be constructed through a public-private partnership in the build-operate-transfer model for PKR 250 billion.[39]

Infrastructure

The motorway cuts through rural areas of southern KP, including underdeveloped districts like Bannu, Tank and Lakki Marwat. The delivery of all three SDGs—education, health, and economic opportunities—is severely limited in these areas. As a result, for healthcare emergencies or specialized education, locals depend on Peshawar or other urban centers in the northern part of the province.[40] At present, options for emergency medical care are limited to three large hospitals—Lady Reading Hospital, Khyber Medical Hospital, and Hayatabad Medical Complex, all in and around Peshawar city, and therefore a considerable distance away from southern KP.[41]

The infrastructure catering to SDG 4 is marginally better. Each district has a public, university. Despite that Several students from Malakand,

Swat, Dir, and Peshawar study at Gomal University in Dera Ismail Khan. The motorway will make these areas more accessible.[42] Others from the area travel to Peshawar regularly, often at great inconvenience. For instance, traveling from D.I. Khan to Peshawar takes eight hours, which can be substantially reduced with the motorway.[43] Similarly, traveling to Peshawar from Karak and Bannu currently takes three hours and can be cut down to under an hour with the proposed motorway.[44] For the entire region, the project promises a direct route that cuts down on travel time, making opportunities for employment, healthcare, and education easily accessible for locals in urban and developing areas.

Transportation is a major source of employment in southern KP. The new motorway is being looked at as a missing link in terms of mobility and connectivity and is expected to assist in the increase of regional trade.[45] Along with a more direct route, an improvement in the quality of infrastructure is expected to reduce the time taken for trucks to travel between cities, decrease turnaround time, and result in an overall improvement in supply chains. The new motorway is expected to encourage the setting up of ancillary industries and facilities for trucks and truckers, further increasing economic opportunities as well as the value of land for locals.[46]

Claims About the Project, and the Reality

As in the case of other major infrastructure projects, the Peshawar–D.I. Khan motorway has attracted significant attention, especially from members of the government and project officials. Former chief minister of KP, Mahmood Khan, has termed the project vital for boosting trade activity with Afghanistan and Central Asia.[47] Shehryar Afridi, former Federal Minister for States and Frontier Regions, has claimed that the motorway would bring employment and tourism opportunities to southern KP and the tribal districts that were recently merged with the province.[48] The provincial government hopes to connect other infrastructure projects in the region with the Peshawar–D.I. Khan motorway and get them recognized as part of the CPEC for easier development and funding opportunities.[49]

Despite a need for better healthcare infrastructure, the current plans for the project do not seem to account for any such facilities. However, the Chinese agency has proposed the construction of several educational institutions along the route of the motorway.[50] Some associated with CPEC projects in the region have pegged the number of schools at as many as 200.[51] They claim that these will include both regular schools as well as technical institutions where Chinese instructors will impart skills to students to increase their employability. This includes a petroleum institute that is expected to be set up in Karak.[52] At a later stage, the government plans to rope in private investors for the upgradation of the schools.[53]

While the authorities claim that the project is on its way to bringing opportunities to the region, some areas of concern remain. Arranging capital for the project seems to be one such issue, with no disclosures being made in either national or provincial legislatures.[54] Though commercial and financial feasibility studies have greenlit the project, local authorities seem unclear on the possible source of the funding.[55] The federal government has reportedly refused to fund the project, and little information on the share of project costs to be borne by the provincial government and Chinese institutions has been made public.[56] Recently, the KP government has allocated some funds to the project, expected to be used for land acquisition.[57]

Response from Citizens and Civil Society

For residents in the region, the greatest draw of the project is its promise to enhance connectivity, increase land prices, and allow the transportation sector to flourish, which is a key source of income for the locals in region. Those associated with the industry expect the Peshawar–D.I. Khan motorway to ensure that consignments reach on time, with less wear and tear on the trucks. Increased activity will bring additional people to the region, giving a boost to the hospitality and service sectors and bringing additional investment to the community.[58] Locals believe that as trade increases, newer markets in Central Asia and Afghanistan will mean more settlements and increased employment opportunities for them.[59] Moreover, the ease of traveling to Peshawar and other urban centers will open new job markets for the locals, especially for unskilled and seasonal ones.[60]

However, a major concern, as in the case of other CPEC projects, has been the lack of clarity on how jobs on the project will be divided between locals and Chinese citizens. Media reports suggest that the Pakistani and Chinese sides have unofficially agreed to an 80-20 split in favor of Pakistan, which means that 80% of the jobs would go to Pakistani citizens, while Chinese employees will only be brought in for roles of technical

Table 5.2 Delivery of Public Goods in KP

Indicator	Rashakai Special Economic Zone	Peshawar–D.I. Khan Motorway
Existing Infrastructure	SDG 3: Preliminary SDG 4: Preliminary SDG 8: Preliminary	SDG 3: Preliminary SDG 4: Advance SDG 8: Preliminary
Access to Existing Infrastructure	SDG 3: Advanced SDG 4: Advanced SDG 8: Preliminary	SDG 3: Preliminary SDG 4: Preliminary SDG 8: Preliminary
Projection of Projects	As a Source of better economic opportunities	As a Source of better socio-economic options
Actual Impact	SDG 3: Small Scale SDG 4: Larger Impact with a Focus on Construction of Technical Institutions SDG 8: To be Determined	SDG 3: To be Determined SDG 4: To be Determined SDG 8: To be Determined
Citizens' Response	SDG 3: Demand for Improved Access SDG 4: Technical Education demanded SDG 8: Local jobs demanded	SDG 3: Demand for Improved Access SDG 4: Demand for Improved Access SDG 8: Local jobs demanded
Miscellaneous	Regional Connectivity with Afghanistan and Refugees' flow may affect the delivery of public goods	Better Connectivity to affect the lives of common people

experts or managers.[61] However, with few skilled people in KP, locals are concerned that they will not be able to make the most of the opportunity as they will only manage to secure jobs as laborers or security personnel, with higher-paying jobs meant for Pakistani citizens being taken up by more qualified people from other provinces like Punjab.[62]

The lack of clarity regarding funding has also led to the concern that it may delay the development of the motorway. The project is expected to take three to four years to complete once started, but locals are worried that the issue may mean that there will be no benefit from the project for the next fifteen to twenty years.[63] Residents say that they are apprehensive that such a development will, in turn, delay all the other projects that are being planned with the assumption that the motorway will be completed on time.[64]

There is considerable excitement about the proposal to set up schools and technical institutes to impart skills to the local community. Residents expect the upskilling to lead to increased employability and eventually add to the socioeconomic progress in the region.[65] However, there is also worry over the fact that there has been no official confirmation of the proposal so far. While political leaders have often mentioned these institutes, there has been no concrete information on where or when they will be set up and the modalities of how they will operate.[66]

In KP the major concern was the delay in the execution and implementation of the CPEC projects which is adding to the public discontent. However, there is prevailing euphoria in the region regarding economic impacts of the CPEC. The findings regarding both RSEZ and Peshawar–D.I. Khan Motorway are being summarized in the Table 5.2.

Notes

1. Shahbaz Rana, "6th Census Findings: 207 Million and Counting," *The Express Tribune*, August 25, 2017, https://tribune.com.pk/story/1490674/57-increase-pakistans-population-19-years-shows-new-census.
2. Please see the official Website of the Government of Khyber Pakhtunkhwa to know more about these policies, https://pndkp.gov.pk/2020/11/30/tribal-decade-strategy-2020-2030/.
3. Rafiullah Kakar, "Making Sense of CPEC Controversary—II," *The Express Tribune*, January 28, 2016, https://tribune.com.pk/story/1035871/making-sense-of-the-cpec-controversy-ii.
4. Brief on CPEC by Planning and Development Department, Government of Khyber Pakhtunkhwa.
5. "Rashakai SEZ: A Harbinger of Prosperous: Pakistan with Potential to Generate over 200,000 Jobs," *The News*, December 27, 2020, https://www.thenews.com.pk/print/765118-rashakai-sez-a-harbinger-of-prosperous-pakistan-with-potential-to-generate-over-200-000-jobs.
6. Ibid.
7. "KP Celebrates Completion of Infrastructure Work on Rashakai SEZ," *Business Recorder*, July 24, 2023, https://www.brecorder.com/news/40254157.

8. "Economy Has Passed Difficult Phase, Says Imran," *The Express Tribune*, May 28, 2021, https://tribune.com.pk/story/2302126/economy-has-passed-difficult-phase-says-imran.
9. "Prime Minister Says Difficult Time Is Over," *The Nation*, May 29, 2021, https://www.nation.com.pk/category/national/page/2912.
10. Interview with Stakeholder D10, May 2021.
11. Interview with Stakeholder D14, July 2021.
12. "Establishment of Rashakai SEZ to Be a Milestone Achievement for Industrial Development in Pakistan, Says Chinese Ambassador," CPEC News, September 12, 2019, https://cpecinfo.com/china-to-help-pakistan-revamp-education-sector-with-modern-e-learning-system/.
13. Interview with Stakeholder B3, May 2021.
14. Interview with Stakeholder D15, June 2021; see Official Website of RSEZ, https://rashakai.com/cpec-city/.
15. Interview with Stakeholder B3, May 2021; Interview with Stakeholder G2, June 2021; Interview with Stakeholder D10, May 2021.
16. Ali Ozgen, "A Step Towards Industrialization," *The News*, April 4, 2021, https://www.thenews.com.pk/tns/detail/814223-a-step-towards-industrialisation.
17. Interview with Stakeholder C8, July 2021.
18. Interview with Stakeholder G2, June 2021.
19. "250,000 People to Get Jobs in Rashakai Economic Zone, CM," *Dawn*, February 23, 2020, https://www.dawn.com/news/1536093; Interview with Stakeholder D15, June 2021; see also Muhammad Arshad, "CPEC's Rashakai Economic Zone to Be a Game Changer for KP," Economy.pk, June 8, 2021, https://www.economy.pk/cpecs-rashakai-economic-zone-to-be-a-game-changer-for-kp/.
20. Interview with Stakeholder B3, May 2021.
21. Interview with Stakeholder A4, June 2021.
22. Interview with Stakeholder D15, June 2021.
23. Interview with Stakeholder B3, May 2021.
24. Interview with Stakeholder B5, June 2021; for more details, see "Special Report: July 2018–February 2021," Special Committee on the Project of China-Pakistan Economic Corridor of the Senate

of Pakistan, accessed March 12, 2022, https://senate.gov.pk/uploads/documents/1618208392_255.pdf.
25. Interview with Stakeholder A5, June 2021; Interview with Stakeholder D10, May 2021.
26. Interview with Stakeholder B2, April 2021.
27. Interview with Stakeholder A7, June 2021.
28. Ejaz Gul and Inam Sharif Chaudhry, "Imminent Prosperity at the Doorsteps of Households: Evidence from Socio-Kinetics of Rashakai Economic Zone Using Dynamic Two Point Model" (Paper Presented at the 33rd Annual General Meeting and Conference of the Pakistan Society of Development Economists, Islamabad, December 12–14, 2017), 385–405, https://file-psde.pide.org.pk/uploads/2017/12/Ejaz%20Gul.pdf.
29. Interview with Stakeholder D9, May 2021.
30. Interview with Stakeholder D15, June 2021.
31. Interview with Stakeholder B2, April 2021.
32. "4491 People Have Been Appointed for CPEC Security," *Nawai Waqt*, April 18, 2017, https://www.nawaiwaqt.com.pk/E-Paper/Islamabad/2017-04-18/page-12/detail-26.
33. Interview with Stakeholder D14, July 2021; Interview with Stakeholder D9, May 2021.
34. Interview with Stakeholder C6, March 2021; Interview with Stakeholder A9, June 2021; Interview with Stakeholder A5, June 2021.
35. Interview with Stakeholder C8, July 2021.
36. Ashfaq Yusufzai, "Health Facilities to Be Improved in Refugee-Hosting Districts," *Dawn*, March 22, 2021, https://www.dawn.com/news/1613839/health-facilities-to-be-improved-in-refugee-hosting-districts.
37. Ministry of Planning Development & Special Initiatives, "CPEC 10th Joint Cooperation Committee Meeting," press release, September 2021, https://www.pc.gov.pk/web/press/get_press/649; see also Associated Press of Pakistan, "Work on CPED Western Route in Full Swing," December 21, 2022, https://www.app.com.pk/business/work-on-cpec-western-route-in-full-swing/.
38. "CPEC Joint Group Adopts Three Road Projects," *The Express Tribune*, October 26, 2020, https://tribune.com.pk/story/2270001/cpec-joint-working-group-adopts-three-road-projects.

39. "Sense of Achievement in KP after Adoption of Its 3 Major Road Projects Under CPEC," *The News*, November 11, 2020, https://www.thenews.com.pk/print/741937-sense-of-achievement-in-kp-after-adoption-of-its-3-major-roads-projects-under-cpec.
40. Interview with Stakeholder A4, June 2021.
41. Interview with Stakeholder A6, June 2021.
42. Interview with Stakeholder A4, June 2021.
43. Interview with Stakeholder A8, June 2021.
44. Interview with Stakeholder A9, June 2021.
45. Interview with Stakeholder A7, June 2021.
46. Interview with Stakeholder B3, May 2021.
47. "CM Wants Swat Motorway and Other Projects Included in CPEC," *The News*, February 20, 2021, https://www.thenews.com.pk/print/792776-cm-wants-swat-motorway-other-projects-included-in-cpec.
48. "399km Peshawar—D.I. Khan Motorway Announced," *Dawn*, December 3, 2019, https://www.dawn.com/news/1520186.
49. Interview with Stakeholder D10, May 2021.
50. Interview with Stakeholder B3, May 2021.
51. Ibid.
52. Interview with Stakeholder D12, June 2021.
53. Interview with Stakeholder B3, May 2021.
54. Interview with Stakeholder D12, June 2021.
55. Interview with Stakeholder A7, June 2021.
56. Mushtaq Ghumman, "Govt Refuses to Finance KPK Motorway Projects," *Business Recorder*, September 24, 2021, https://www.brecorder.com/news/40122336.
57. "KP Presents 1.1tr, "Balanced Budget," *The Express Tribune*, June 19, 2021, https://tribune.com.pk/story/2306048/k-p-presents-11tr-balanced-budget.
58. Interview with Stakeholder B3, May 2021.
59. Interview with Stakeholder A4, July 2021.
60. Interview with Stakeholder D12, June 2021.
61. Interview with Stakeholder D12, June 2021.
62. Interview with Stakeholder A7, June 2021.
63. Interview with Stakeholder C8, July 2021.
64. Interview with Stakeholder D14, July 2021.
65. Interview with Stakeholder D12, June 2021.
66. Interview with Stakeholder A8, June 2021.

CHAPTER 6

CPEC and the Delivery of Public Goods in Punjab

Abstract This chapter examines the impacts of the Sahiwal Coal Power Plant and the Orange Line Metro Train (OLMT) projects in Punjab—the biggest and mostly urbanized province in Pakistan. These CPEC projects are completed and functional. While both projects seemed to have accelerated urbanization process, a well-thought-out plan to provide jobs, increase productivity, ensure smooth public service delivery, and provide high living standards, was found absent in both Lahore and Sahiwal. The SDGs 3, 4 and 8 received little attention while planning the CPEC in Punjab.

Keywords Sahiwal Coal Power Plant · Orange Line Metro Train (OLMT) · CPEC · Punjab · Lahore · Sahiwal

Introduction

Punjab, as the most populated province of Pakistan, has usually attracted the greatest share of government resources. This has continued under the China-Pakistan Economic Corridor (CPEC), where, along with Sindh, most projects in the first phase were initiated in the province. Out of 122 CPEC projects, thirty-two were completed by 2020.[1] Of the seventeen projects announced for the second phase of the initiative, sixteen are slated for the province.[2] Punjab is also significant as it has rapidly urbanized in recent years, with 37% of its population now living in urban areas.[3] The two projects in this study differ from the others in that they are in primarily urban settings and completed and functional.

The Sahiwal Coal Power Plant and the Orange Line Metro Train (OLMT) projects have both been completed and are functional. The Sahiwal Coal Power Plant project is situated close to Lahore while OLMT is in Lahore, which is the second fastest urbanizing location in the country. The analysis in this case benefits from the perspective of the respondents who can reflect on their expectations of change in public goods delivery after the completion of CPEC projects and whether these expectations have been fulfilled.

SAHIWAL COAL POWER PLANT PROJECT

The Sahiwal Coal Power Plant was built as part of the CPEC by a consortium of China's state-owned Huaneng Group and Shandong Ruyi Technology Group Ltd., with both having a 50-50 stake.[4] It was one of the first CPEC projects in the country that started construction in July 2015 and came online in phases, with 660 megawatts initially and additional 1320 megawatts in 2017.[5] According to the signed agreement, the Pakistan government would purchase electricity from the consortium for thirty years, after which the ownership of the plant would be transferred to the Government of Punjab.

Infrastructure

The Sahiwal Coal Power Plant is on the outskirts of Sahiwal, an urban center with a population of around 2.5 million. Three major cities, Lahore, Faisalabad, and Multan, are less than 200 kilometers away—a key reason for the selection of the location for the plant. Being close to major urban centers, Sahiwal has an adequate healthcare infrastructure, including specialized healthcare. The city also has major educational institutions, including those catering to higher education. Additionally, being connected to major cities by rail and road ensures that residents of the city can access facilities in these cities. However, Sahiwal has also suffered the negative impacts of being well-connected. Railways connecting Sahiwal are used to bring in thousands of tons of coal from Karachi for this plant, which moves through populated areas in open carriages, leading to coal dust mixing with the air and causing a major health hazard.[6]

Claims About the Project, and the Reality

The plant has led people moving to Sahiwal, which has put considerable pressure on the health, education, and economic infrastructure of the city. Additionally, locals claim that the plant has increased the incidence of respiratory and waterborne diseases that need to be tackled. Waste from the plant is believed to have contaminated local freshwater sources, resulting in diseases like Hepatitis C and liver failure.[7] Studies have also indicated that effluents from the plant in groundwater are responsible for increased dental problems among children in the area.[8] Fumes and particulate matter emitted by the plant have increased cases of lung diseases and asthma among locals.[9]

However, on the ground, there is limited focus on health-related initiatives. Residents report that while there were promises of new hospitals, schools, and technical institutes in Sahiwal with the cooperation of Chinese companies, none of them have come to fruition.[10] The power plant management company has signed a corporate social responsibility agreement and a technical training agreement with the provincial government that requires them to pay PKR 200 million per annum to the Punjab government for social welfare, including medical aid and clean drinking water programs for local communities. Beyond the agreements, no step has been taken by the consortium to mitigate the adverse effects of the plant on the citizens' health. Local authorities admit that while attempts should have been made to improve the medical infrastructure in the city because of the impact of the project on health, no such steps have been taken.[11] No new link roads have been constructed to increase the accessibility of the people living inside or in the vicinity of the project to reach already existing health facilities in Sahiwal.

Despite expectations that new educational institutions will be set up as part of the overall development of the area adjoining the plant, there has been little development in the years after the plant came online. The only development has been the setting up of a school inside the project by the Chinese companies to provide language and technical training for local communities, with the expectation that they will find employment in the plant.[12] However, beyond this, the local administration has shifted responsibility to the provincial authorities, claiming that issues like health and education are under the Punjab government and that they should be working independently of CPEC projects to improve the state of delivery of public goods.[13]

The power plant has increased economic opportunities for the residents of Sahiwal to an extent. Approximately 3000 locals were hired during the construction of the plant. At present, about half of the employees are believed to be Pakistani citizens, many of them locals. About 200 Pakistani engineers have received technical training to work on the project.[14] However, the setting up of the plant has, in many ways, upended the traditional socioeconomic setup of the region by acquiring agricultural land for the project. While people who gave up their land were compensated monetarily, a lack of attention to the changes to the overall structure of the local economy and traditional way of life has left a deep impact.[15] Women have been particularly impacted as they were employed in agricultural work. With the land being taken over, they have lost their source of employment along with being displaced from the land without adequate arrangements for rehabilitation.[16] Local civil society activists believe that in many cases, the government acquired farming land for less than the market price.[17] Many of the sellers attempted to shift occupations from farming to opening and running small businesses. However, in the absence of training or support, many of these have failed to take off.[18] The concern, in the absence of coordinated efforts to improve the condition of local people, is the imminent crisis once the compensation money runs out.[19]

Response from Citizens and Civil Society

Locals in Sahiwal are currently undecided if the positives from the power plant in their backyard match up to the negatives. In the run-up to the construction, local politicians and those associated with the project promised overall development, a better quality of life, and jobs for a large number of residents. The project was supposed to attract other development projects as well as solve the problem of inadequate supply of electricity in the region. However, no arrangement has been made with the company running the power plant to ensure that locals get electricity first.[20] Moreover, the electricity produced in the plant is too expensive for many, who have complained that domestic energy costs have skyrocketed for them.[21]

Beyond electricity for all, the Sahiwal plant was expected to bring in a wave of industry and development in the region. However, the standalone plant with no new infrastructure has affected that prospect as well. Despite the availability of electricity, industries have been discouraged by the lack of other infrastructures like motorways to connect Sahiwal to other major urban and industrial centers.[22] Citizens and civil society groups have now accused the provincial and federal governments of politicking over the project for credit, with little concern for the residents.[23] With traditional means of employment unavailable after the acquisition of agricultural land, there is now an increasing demand for the setting up of promised engineering universities and technical institutes.[24]

Local citizens have also questioned why so few of them have been employed by the plant despite promises.[25] They accuse the local government of allowing the Chinese consortium to take all calls regarding the running of the plant and employment, which has ensured that most high-paying positions of managers and technical personnel stay with Chinese citizens.[26] They claim that by the time the plant is handed over to the Punjab government, it would have gone through most of its life cycle, leaving Pakistani engineers and local people to run an old and inefficient project.[27] Civil society groups have already voiced concerns about the technology and machinery used in the project, which is inefficient and below international standards.[28] They claim that the technology requires using cheaper coal, which increases the production cost of electricity and is more polluting. They claim that complaints of respiratory illnesses, allergies, and diseases like asthma and cancer have increased since the setting up of the project and that the government needs to act to improve public health facilities whose provision has been delayed.

The Sahiwal Coal Power Plant has expanded the industrial base of Punjab but at the cost of a clean environment and agricultural livelihood. People currently seem disillusioned with the project in regard to how it has contributed to their wellbeing. In a city of more than two million people, only a few thousand have benefited from jobs in the plant, while many others have not only lost their land but have also been left clueless about how to operate in the changing environment. It is also apparent that promises of better health, education, and economic opportunities that were made in the early stages of the project were guided by political considerations without any concrete backing from the government or the consortium in charge of the plant.

Orange Line Metro Train Project

The Orange Line Metro Train (OLMT) in Lahore, which was announced in 2014 and began operating in October 2020, is a flagship project for the Government of Pakistan, both to showcase the CPEC as well as demonstrate the capability to execute technologically advanced major infrastructure projects that are equipped to address the challenges of rapid urbanization. It is the country's first metro train line as well as one of the first projects to be developed as part of the CPEC. It was constructed by the China North Industries and funded by the federal government as well as with a soft loan of PKR 165 billion from the Export-Import Bank of China.[29] With 27 kilometers of track and twenty-six stations, the route is expected to serve 250,000 passengers daily.[30] The project aims to enhance the mobility of the people of Lahore and offer them a safe, efficient, comfortable, environment-friendly, and economical mode of daily travel.

Infrastructure

As a project in the heart of one of the most populated cities in Pakistan with established systems of delivery of health and education services and multiple means of employment, the challenges for the OLMT were different from the other projects in this study. The project was not expected to create fresh avenues for the delivery of public goods but to facilitate the optimization of existing mechanisms. Stakeholders have highlighted the role of the OLMT in improving mobility and connectivity to health facilities, educational institutions, and places of employment. According to them, for those arriving in Lahore through Thokar Niaz Baig, one of the key entrance points to the city, the OLMT allows access to hospitals, educational institutes, courts, and other commercial areas along the route of the metro.[31] During construction, the project's real challenge was found to be elsewhere—in facilitating access to existing public goods without impacting the rich historical heritage of the city, which is not only key to the cultural identity of the region but is also important for the tourism industry, which is a major employer.[32] Conservationists and civil society have been united in this demand from the time of the project's introduction, leading to the matter being taken up by the Supreme Court of the country in 2016.[33]

Claims About the Project, and the Reality

At the launch of the project, the chief minister claimed that the project was the government's attempt to provide world-class facilities to the citizens of Pakistan and a significant step toward advances in urban development.[34] The metro, weaving through the most densely populated parts of the city, would improve access to major educational institutions like Punjab University and M.A.O College as well as major hospitals like Ganga Ram Hospital and Mayo Hospital.[35] The project also brought with it promises of improved employment. The Chinese consul general in Lahore claimed that the project had already employed 7000 locals and would employ 2000 more in operation and maintenance roles.[36] Parts of the city, such as those close to Gulshani Ravi, Lakshmi Chowk, and Niaz Baig stations, became more accessible because of the metro, allowing people opportunities to expand their businesses and multiply their economic options.[37]

However, a lot of these opportunities have remained unfulfilled. The most significant issue has been the construction of the metro line without adequate attention to other modes of connectivity like Speedo buses and other public transport.[38] The promise of connecting the line to major industrial bases and employment hubs in and around the city has also remained unfulfilled, leading to the project not living up to its potential.[39] Similarly, despite the promise of increasing economic options, the project has caused a shrinking of economic opportunities. Businesses in areas that are now along the OLMT track (for instance, near the Lakshmi Chowk station) were either demolished for metro construction or have become less accessible. Few of the affected have been compensated by the authorities.[40]

As in the case of other CPEC projects, the number of jobs created as part of the project falls short of promises. Local authorities claim that the project has created more than 250 jobs in technical or engineering roles for locals.[41] However, despite this, most experts and managers are hired from China as the consortium of Chinese companies—consisting of Guangzhou Metro and NORINCO International—which oversees technical and operational aspects of the project prefer them. Almost all Pakistani nationals working with the OLMT are engaged in roles that require manual labor or guarding the assets of the project.[42] While the management of the project is supposed to be handed over to Pakistani agencies after completing eight years of operations, technical institutes or workshops to train the local workforce are yet to be set up.[43]

Response from Citizens and Civil Society

The project has evinced mixed reactions from the local population. While the option of a modern, non-polluting, and efficient mode of public transport is attractive, citizens believe that the project was rushed due to political considerations, leading to gaps in design that reduce the efficacy of the service. A major example illustrating this can be found in the controversy surrounding the effect of the project on Lahore's many heritage sites. Soon after the project was announced in 2015, civil society groups protested the risk that the metro posed to Shalimar Gardens, a seventeenth-century complex that is among the top tourist attractions of the country.[44]

The controversy soon became political, with opposition parties claiming that the government was obfuscating details of the agreement between China and Pakistan on the project and demanding that the matter be discussed in the provincial legislature.[45] Soon after, civil society groups and activists organized protests against the plans for the metro, claiming that the government was ignoring their demands to protect heritage sites.[46] The matter eventually reached the Lahore High Court, which, in 2016, suspended construction of the OLMT within 200 feet of eleven heritage sites and found issues with the no objection certificate for the project.[47] Finally, in 2018, the Supreme Court of Pakistan constituted a committee of experts to oversee the project and ensure all protected monuments near the project were safeguarded.[48]

Another example that highlights the lack of adequate planning is reflected in the relative inaccessibility of the metro stations. The fact that the OLMT and the city's bus service are designed almost entirely independently has been a major issue for most commuters.[49] In the absence of shuttles that connect to the metro station, many find the metro too expensive to use regularly, especially if they have to avail other public transportation to reach metro stations.[50] Others have pointed out that the cost of using the metro, which is set at PKR 40 (USD 0.20), may be high for large sections of society and does not fulfill the promise of offering affordable means of transport to everyone to reach their areas of work.[51]

There has also been considerable debate on whether the metro line should have been a priority given other development challenges for Lahore. The OLMT ran on a loss of PKR 900 million in its first few

Table 6.1 Delivery of Public Goods in Punjab

Indicator	Sahiwal Coal Power Plant	Orange Line Metro Train
Existing Infrastructure	SDG 3: Advanced SDG 4: Advanced SDG 8: Advanced	SDG 3: Advanced SDG 4: Advanced SDG 8: Advanced
Access to Existing Infrastructure	SDG 3: Preliminary SDG 4: Preliminary SDG 8: Preliminary	SDG 3: Preliminary SDG 4: Preliminary SDG 8: Preliminary
Projection of Projects	As a Source of better economic opportunities	Fast and Cheap Transportation
Actual Impact	SDG 3: No Substantial Impact SDG 4: No Substantial Impact SDG 8: No Substantial Impact	SDG 3: No Substantial Impact SDG 4: No Substantial Impact SDG 8: No Substantial Impact
Citizens' Response	SDG 3: Better Health Infrastructure SDG 4: Technical Education demanded SDG 8: Local jobs demanded	SDG 3: Connectivity to Health Infrastructure SDG 4: Connectivity to Education Infrastructure SDG 8: Local jobs demanded
Miscellaneous	Environmental Concerns played a key role in delivery of public goods	Impact on cultural heritage and shrinking of existing economic and business opportunities due to poor planning

months.[52] This coincides with the decision by the provincial government to allocate PKR 5 billion from its limited budget as a subsidy to the OLMT project.[53] This has raised questions about whether the needs of a rapidly growing city like Lahore would have been met better with improved medical facilities or additional facilities for schools and colleges.[54] Even projects that were started before the OLMT, such as sports facilities, roadways, and waste management initiatives, have been suspended as resources were diverted toward the metro line.[55] The opposition parties demanded that the authorities assure the people of Lahore that funds earmarked for other purposes were not being used up for the metro project.[56]

The analysis of the two projects in Punjab suggests some key dissimilarities with those in rural Pakistan. The relatively improved infrastructure and other facilities in the province allowed development with relatively fewer interruptions. However, as in KP or AJK, there was little attention on linking CPEC projects to the overall wellbeing of communities. No significant impact of the projects was found in the health or education sectors either in either Sahiwal or Lahore. The government seemed keen to promise employment as a political message irrespective of the existence of an actual plan. While both projects seemed to accelerate urbanization, a well-thought-out plan to provide jobs, increase productivity, ensure smooth public service delivery, and provide high living standards, was absent.

Table 6.1 summarizes the situation on the ground regarding the attainments of SDGs 3, 4 and 8 and how do the people of Lahore and Sahiwal view this project.

Notes

1. Jonathan E. Hillman and Maesea McCalpin, "The China-Pakistan Economic Corridor at Five," Center for Strategic and International Studies, April 2020, https://www.csis.org/analysis/china-pakistan-economic-corridor-five.
2. Nasir Jamal, "S Punjab to Get Major Share of Uplift Schemes Under CPEC," *Dawn*, March 14, 2019, https://www.dawn.com/news/1469439.
3. Rana, "6th Census Findings: 207 Million and Counting."
4. Muhammad Muzammil Zia and Shujaa Waqar, "Sahiwal Coal Power Plant "Exploring Employment and Environmental Effects"," April 2018, https://cpec-centre.pk/wp-content/uploads/2018/06/Sahiwal-Case-Study.pdf.
5. "PM Will Inaugurate 2 Coal Power Plants of 660 MW in Sahiwal," *Nawai Waqt*, May 30, 2014, https://www.nawaiwaqt.com.pk/E-Paper/islamabad/2014-05-30; "1320 MW Power Generated from Sahiwal Coal Power Project," *Nawai Waqt*, June 3, 2017, https://www.nawaiwaqt.com.pk/E-Paper/Islamabad/2017-06-03/page-1/detail-19.
6. Azhar Lashari, "A Dirty, Deadly Business," *The News*, August 18, 2019, https://www.thenews.com.pk/tns/detail/568327-dirty-deadly-business.
7. Syed Muhammad Abubakar, "Life Under the Shadow of a Coal-Fired Power Plant," *Dawn*, December 22, 2019, https://www.dawn.com/news/1522388.

8. Interview with Stakeholder D4, February 2021.
9. Komal Niazi, "Environmental Impact of the Sahiwal Coal Power Plant," *The Daily Times*, September 21, 2018, https://dailytimes.com.pk/300805/environmental-impact-of-the-sahiwal-coal-power-plant/; Syed Muhammad Abubakar, "Life Under the Shadow of a Coal-Fired Power Plant," *Dawn*, December 22, 2019, https://www.dawn.com/news/1522388.
10. Interview with Stakeholder C5, March 2021.
11. Ibid.
12. Abdul Rauf, "Sahiwal Coal-Fired Power Plant," *Pivot* 2, no.1 (January 2020); see also Belt and Road Initiative, "Sahiwal Coal Power Project," https://www.beltroad-initiative.com/sahiwal-coal-power-project/#more-1776; Numra Asif, Saleem Janjua, and Adnan Khan, "Analysing Environmental Impacts for Coal-Fired Power Plants Under CPEC," CPEC Center of Excellence, CPEC Working Paper Series, no. 3, 2018; Interview with Stakeholder D6, February 2021.
13. Interview with Stakeholder C4, February 2021.
14. Interview with Stakeholder D5, February 2021.
15. Interview with Stakeholder D6, February 2021.
16. Komal Niazi, Guoqiang He, and Shakir Ullah, "Lifestyle Change of Female Farmers Through CPEC's Coal Power Plant Project Initiative," *Journal of International Women's Studies* 20, no. 3 (2019): 154–67.
17. Interview with Stakeholder D2, February 2021.
18. Interview with Stakeholder C4, February 2021.
19. Interview with Stakeholder D4, February 2021.
20. Interview with Stakeholder D5, February 2021.
21. Interview with Stakeholder D2, February 2021.
22. Interview with Stakeholder A3, March 2021.
23. Interview with Stakeholder A1, December 2020.
24. Interview with Stakeholder A3, March 2021.
25. Interview with Stakeholder C5, March 2021.
26. Interview with Stakeholder D4, February 2021.
27. Interview with Stakeholder D2, February 2021.
28. Interview with Stakeholder A3, March 2021.

29. Imran Adnan, "Infrastructure Project: First Tranche of OLMT Loan Released," *The Express Tribune*, May 11, 2016, https://tribune.com.pk/story/1101837/infrastructure-project-first-tranche-of-olmt-loan-released.
30. Sabrinna Topa, "Lahore Metro Brings Uncertainty for Displaced Residents," *Dawn*, December 23, 2020, https://www.dawn.com/news/1597333; Interview with Stakeholder D8, March 2021.
31. Interview with Stakeholder G1, December 2020.
32. Interview with Stakeholder A1, December 2020.
33. Abira Ashfaq, "Orange Line Metro: Will the Supreme Court Save Lahore's Heritage," *Dawn*, October 13, 2016, https://www.dawn.com/news/1289715.
34. Ahsan Zia, "Much ado About OLMT," *The News*, November 1, 2020, https://www.thenews.com.pk/tns/detail/736996-much-ado-about-olmt.
35. Interview with Stakeholder D3, February 2021.
36. Yasir Habi Khan, "Metro Train Lahore, a Gift from China," *China Today*, November 5, 2020, http://www.chinatoday.com.cn/ctenglish/2018/ii/202011/t20201105_800226035.html.
37. Nabeel Shakeel, "Highlighting the Potentials of Transit Oriented Development: A Case Study of Orange Line Metro Train, Lahore," Proceedings of the 2019 World Transport Convention, Beijing, China, June 13–16, 2019, https://www.academia.edu/41138690/Highlighting_the_Potentials_of_Transit_Oriented_Development_A_Case_Study_of_Orange_Line_Metro_Train_Lahore.
38. Interview with Stakeholder J1, December 2020.
39. Interview with Stakeholder A3, March 2021.
40. Anam Hussain, "Running Over the Ruins of My Home: Lahore's Orange Train," Al Jazeera, December 1, 2020, https://www.aljazeera.com/features/2020/12/1/pakistan-lahore-orange-train; see also Sabrina Topa, "'This Will Make Us Poorer': Pakistani Metro Brings Uncertainty for Displaced Residents," Reuters, December 22, 2020, https://www.reuters.com/article/us-pakistan-lahore-metro-feature-idUSKBN28W039.
41. Interview with Stakeholder C3, January 2021.
42. Interview with Stakeholder D8, March 2021.
43. Interview with Stakeholder H3, February 2021.

44. "Orange Line Metro Train and the Threats It Poses to World Heritage Sites," Global Village Space, June 17, 2017, https://www.globalvillagespace.com/orange-line-metro-train-and-the-threats-it-poses-to-world-heritage-sites/.
45. Aroosa Shaukat, "Up in Arms: Opposition Parties Plan Orange Line Protests Next week," *The Express Tribune*, January 28, 2016, https://tribune.com.pk/story/1035984/up-in-arms-opposition-parties-plan-orange-line-protest-next-week.
46. "Orange Line Project: Government Warned of Massive Protests," *Dawn*, December 12, 2015, https://www.dawn.com/news/1225800. Like Ausaf, I do not have the web source to confirm what the actual news is.
47. Abira Ashfaq, "Orange Line Metro: Will the Supreme Court Save Lahore's Heritage," *Dawn*, October 13, 2016, https://www.dawn.com/news/1289715.
48. "Safety Measures at Monuments Satisfactory on Metro Train Route," *The News*, January 13, 2018, https://www.thenews.com.pk/print/267860-safety-measures-at-monuments-satisfactory-on-metro-train-route.
49. Interview with Stakeholder A3, March 2021.
50. Interview with Stakeholder D3, February 2021.
51. Ibid.
52. Aamir Naveed, "OLMT Losses Keep Accumulating in Punjab," *The Express Tribune*, March 8, 2021, https://tribune.com.pk/story/2288077/olmt-losses-keep-accumulating-in-punjab.
53. Interview with Stakeholder J1, December 2020.
54. Interview with Stakeholder D1, December 2020.
55. Ibid.
56. Aroosa Shaukat, "Up in Arms: Opposition Parties Plan Orange Line Protests Next Week," *The Express Tribune*, January 28, 2016, https://tribune.com.pk/story/1035984/up-in-arms-opposition-parties-plan-orange-line-protest-next-week.

CHAPTER 7

Conclusion and Recommendations

Abstract This chapter after analyzing six CPEC projects in both rural and urban areas of Pakistan reach to the conclusion that the delivery of better health or education infrastructure or other public goods is not tied to the core objectives of CPEC projects. The focus on promise, expectation, and creation of economic opportunities (SDG 8) is a common thread running through all projects in Punjab, AJK and KP, however, there is least of an attention given to health and education sectors (SDG 3 and 4) in CPEC. The study recommends giving due consideration to the people's needs in the areas of health (SDG 3), education (SDG 4) and economic wellbeing (SDG 8) while implementing various projects. Such an approach would ensure sustainable development of the CPEC through making it more inclusive and people-centric project.

Keywords CPEC · Pakistan · People-centric · SDGs · Health · Education · Economic wellbeing

The China-Pakistan Economic Corridor (CPEC) has remained one of the major development initiatives in Pakistan despite its slow pace and stalled progress in the past few years. Various CPEC projects have expanded geographically across the country. This has also resulted in the diversification of projects not only geographically but also in a sectorial manner.

© The Author(s), under exclusive license to Springer Nature Switzerland AG 2024
S. Sulaiman, *The CPEC and SDGs in Pakistan*,
https://doi.org/10.1007/978-3-031-65579-1_7

However, this study finds that the CPEC so far has existed independent of the national development objectives and policies of Pakistan. For example, while the national development strategy is guided by two major considerations—the primarily agrarian nature of Pakistani society and major urbanization—CPEC projects have been focused on developing communication infrastructure, industrialization, the energy sector, and transportation. While the two sets of objectives converge in certain instances, identifying the divergences and acting on the same can assist in realizing the full potential of the CPEC. Major inferences from the study can be categorized as below.

SDG Delivery Is Not a Core Objective for CPEC Projects at Present

Delivery of better health or education infrastructure or other public goods is not tied to the core objectives of CPEC projects that were part of this study and started in the first phase of the initiative. As expressed on the official website of the CPEC these early projects were guided toward removing existing bottlenecks and ensuring favorable conditions for future economic development. However, big infrastructure projects, by their very nature, disrupt existing socioeconomic structures. In Sahiwal, for example, not only has the project interrupted agricultural practices, but it has also disenfranchised a large number of women who were employed in the sector. Such developments have long-term ramifications across the fabric of society—a fact that needs to be acknowledged and understood.

CPEC Projects Aid SDG 8 More Than SDG 3 or SDG 4

The focus on promise, expectation, and creation of economic opportunities is a common thread running through all projects examined in this study. Politicians, elected representatives, and bureaucrats alike emphasized the role of CPEC projects in creating jobs for residents of the area. Simultaneously, local people expected that the projects would lead to mass employment, irrespective of whether their skillsets matched those required in these projects or not. In most cases, CPEC projects automatically resulted in the multiplication of economic opportunities. At times, these would direct recruitment as manual laborers or security personnel; at other times, this would include business opportunities indirectly linked with the CPEC projects, such as shops and truck stops along newly constructed CPEC highways. Even in challenging places like AJK, people were found cautiously optimistic about the eventual possibility of increased employment.

However, the projects, in certain cases have disturbed existing economic systems without arranging for alternatives. The acquisition of arable land for projects is a common refrain; in the case of the NJHP, the Kohala Hydropower Plant, and the Sahiwal Coal Power Plant, adverse impacts on water sources and air quality have also had economic impacts. Finally, while people are hopeful of being employed by the projects, an equal number of them are concerned that all high-paying jobs in the project are given to Chinese nationals. Some believe that this is unlikely to change before the projects are handed to Pakistani entities after running for some years, by which time, the projects would already be near the end of their life cycle.[1]

For SDG 3 and SDG 4, the Promised Effect of CPEC Projects Does Not Match the Reality

As explained earlier, the delivery of public goods is not a core objective for CPEC projects. Most of the projects claim to have plans for skill development. For instance, technical institutes to train the local people were part of the plan for the Sahiwal Coal Power Plant. In the RSEZ, there is a plan to link the project with technical institutes in the vicinity to train manpower for various industries in the SEZ. Even the proposal for the Kohala Hydropower Plant focused on promoting technical education as part of the project. However, these promises are often found to be left unfulfilled. In many cases, instead of upskilling the local population, the Chinese companies in charge of the projects have met the need for skilled laborers by bringing them from China.

There has been little focus on health facilities as well. All sites are equipped with small health units with limited health facilities for workers and their families. In most cases, these facilities also cater to the local population. However, despite promises being made as part of community investment programs, those in charge of the projects do not seem to have focused on constructing bigger health facilities or specialized medical infrastructure. Even in the case of the OLMT, little attention was paid to linking up the metro line with key hospitals across Lahore.

CPEC Projects Affect Urban and Rural Areas Differently

The study finds critical differences in the ways that people in rural and urban Pakistan expect CPEC projects to bring changes in the delivery of health, education, and economic opportunities. In urban areas with preexisting infrastructure and greater awareness, the projects were expected to address questions of access, as in the case of the OLMT connecting universities and hospitals in Lahore. A common complaint against the project pertained to the problem of accessing the metro train in the absence of feeder buses or the disconnection of the metro from the bus system. However, in rural areas, civil society and citizens expected the projects to help establish new facilities. Moreover, in areas like AJK and KP, protests and demands surrounding CPEC projects focused more on disruptions brought about by the projects, such as falling levels of river water and inadequate compensation for land, than on the promises of new infrastructure that were not fulfilled. In rural areas, the CPEC is associated largely with the possibility of employment, whereas in urban areas, CPEC projects are looked at more holistically—as conduits for better health and education facilities along with employment opportunities.

Table 7.1 provides a detailed description of the findings from both the urban and rural area projects in terms of CPEC impacts on SDGs 3, 4, and 8.

Policy Recommendations

Considering the findings, the study offers the following policy recommendations.

   a Establishing Link between CPEC and SDGs
      Despite the commitment to SDGs by both China and Pakistan, better delivery of SDG goals is currently not at the core of CPEC projects. With the initiation of the second phase of the CPEC, project planning and investment policies must clearly identify SDG targets, including health, education, and an increase in employment

7 CONCLUSION AND RECOMMENDATIONS 91

Table 7.1 Impact of CPEC Projects on SDGs

	Neelum-Jhelum Hydroelectric Plant	Kohala Hydroelectric Plant	Rashakai Special Economic Zone	Peshawar–D.I. Khan Motorway	Sahiwal Coal Power Plant	Orange Line Metro Train
SDG 3—Health	Partially met—slight focus on health infrastructure	Partially met—slight focus on health infrastructure development	Partially achieved—accessibility and mobility to the health infrastructure	Partially achieved—focus on connectivity and mobility in terms of access to health facilities	Not met—least focus on health despite acute health consequences	Not met—least focus on health infrastructure development and connectivity as well
SDG 4—Education	Partially met—focus on technical education	Partially met—focus on technical education	Partially met—focus on technical education	To be determined	Partially met—focus on technical education	Partially met—focus on access to education infrastructure
SDG 8—Economic Wellbeing	Met—key focus on multiplication of economic opportunities through infrastructural development to improve quality of life	Met—key focus on multiplication of economic opportunities through infrastructural development to improve quality of life	Met—key focus on multiplication of economic opportunities through infrastructural development to improve quality of life	Met—key focus on multiplication of economic opportunities through increased mobility and connectivity to improve quality of life	Met—key focus on multiplication of economic opportunities through infrastructural development to improve quality of life	Met—key focus on multiplication of economic opportunities through better mobility and connectivity to improve quality of life

opportunities. This can only be done if addressing SDG delivery is one of the core objectives of the projects. For example, a highways project must not consider connecting two places as its only goal. It must prioritize connecting public goods infrastructure with the newly constructed highway and account for the possible need to invest in new facilities as per the project budget and timelines.

b Fulfilling Promises of Public Service Delivery

Authorities at the local and federal levels must ensure that agencies tasked with CPEC projects live up to their promises of the delivery of public goods. This has not been the case despite the existence of community investment programs, as in the case of AJK. In Punjab, consortiums managing CPEC projects are required to pay a fixed amount annually for social welfare, with no other responsibilities. Both these models have failed to meet the needs of local communities. Therefore, agreements between Pakistani authorities and Chinese entities need to specify the responsibilities of the project developers and hold them accountable.

c Inclusion of Local People

Upskilling of local populations to ensure that they are employable in CPEC projects must be prioritized. Despite promises to set up technical training facilities on or near CPEC projects as well as connect them to existing facilities, this aspect addressing SDG 8 requirements has often remained unfulfilled. As a result, Chinese companies developing and running projects have been able to justify meeting their human resource needs by bringing in Chinese citizens to fulfill these roles. An adequate focus on training members of the local labor force can ensure that they are equipped to fulfill these responsibilities, be it as managers and engineers or laborers with specific skills.

d. People's Friendly Development

CPEC projects must acknowledge the disruption that big projects cause to existing ways of life and develop plans to mitigate them. For instance, the location of the Sahiwal project has made it difficult for locals to travel between villages. Similarly, communities in AJK have been affected by the environmental impact of the projects. In Lahore, the construction of tracks for the OLMT has displaced traders. In almost all rural projects, long-term economic practices like agriculture have been interrupted due to large-scale land acquisition. These disturbances to the social fabric need to be understood and plans for alternatives need to be included in the early stages of planning a project.

The CPEC has yet to go a long way, hence giving due consideration to the people's needs and requirements while implementing various projects would ensure sustainable development. Pakistan is faced with toughest choices due to the persistent economic and political challenges as discussed in the study and CPEC can be helpful in mitigating some of them, subject to internal efforts and reforms by government of Pakistan. However, such state initiatives would need the backing and support by the people for ensuring sustainable stability. Therefore, popular perceptions regarding such initiatives as big as CPEC needs due attention and consideration, otherwise the impact can be confined and limited in scope and effectiveness.

Note

1. Interview with Stakeholder D2, February 2021.

Index

A
access, 9
administrative unit, 45
Agenda 2030, 2
Agriculture, 23
Azad Jammu and Kashmir, 45

C
China-Pakistan Economic Corridor, v
Citizens, 10
civil society, 10
coal, 77
Communities, v
connectivity, 1
construction, 1

D
Decent work, 2

E
Early Harvest Projects, 19
economic debt, 4

energy, 17, 19
energy deficit, 4
environmental degradation, 52
existing infrastructure, 6
external debt, 40

G
gender equality, 33
geopolitics, 2
Gwadar Port, 3, 22

H
health infrastructure, 35
higher education, 74
highways, 6
historical heritage, 78
hospital, 50

I
industrial growth, 18
infrastructure, 17, 20
Investment, vi

K
Kohala Hydropower Project, 59
Kohala Hydropower Project, 45, 46, 49

L
living standards, 9
Local communities, vi
lung diseases, 75

M
M1 motorway, 61
metro line, 80
mortality rates, 35

N
Neelum Jhelum Hydroelectric Project, 45, 46

O
Orange Line Metro Train, 78
Out of School Children, 37

P
Pakistan, vi
Peshawar, 59
Peshawar–D.I. Khan motorway, 65
public goods, 2
public-private partnership, 61

R
Rashakai Special Economic Zone, 60

S
Sahiwal Coal Power Plant, 74
Save the Rivers, 49
Science and Technology, 23
socioeconomic, 23
Special Economic Zones, 21
sustainable development, 2
Sustainable Development Goals, vi

T
transport, 3
transportation, 17, 20

U
urbanization, 3

W
waste management, 81

Printed in the United States
by Baker & Taylor Publisher Services